If you run from 'minor proph
be impractical, like walking
you to read Tim Chester's en
is no shortage of good sch<

thoroughness, Tim constantly shows how the message of
Hosea relates to the gospel of Jesus, and especially how the
prophet's challenges to decadent Israel are as up to date as the 6
o'clock news. This fresh, readable, insightful commentary will
lead you to worship a God who is jealous for our affections,
and loves us too much to leave us sitting comfortably in
apathy! Jargon free study questions make it useful for small
groups, as well as preachers wanting to know what the text
means, and how to apply it clearly. I wish all commentaries
followed this model, and brought the ancient truth of God's
Word through our front door on a Monday morning. Tim is
a great example of a pastor/scholar who knows he has not
been faithful to the text until it is wrestling with our hearts in
today's world. Preachers, Bible study leaders and all thinking
Christians cannot fail to profit from this sound and exciting
read.

Jeremy McQuoid
Teaching Pastor
Deeside Christian Fellowship
Aberdeen, Scotland

This is an excellent commentary on an under-preached
part of God's word. It is exegetically faithful so that there is
a clear sense of what this would have meant to Hosea and
his contemporaries. Moreover, it treats Hosea as Christian
Scripture, and each part of the commentary takes us clearly to
the Lord Jesus. This book has deepened my love for the One
who first loved me, and I think it is a valuable addition to the
existing commentaries on Hosea.

Robin Weekes
Minister
Emmanuel Church Wimbledon
London

In his commentary Tim Chester has left few scholarly stones unturned yet we are not invited to behave as academic spectators on the text. In these pages we find Israel's sin set out in graphic detail but not so we might disapprove. The drama is placed within the bigger picture of the whole bible; difficult issues are not avoided and the prophet's ministry is unerringly allowed to leads us to Christ. However the great strength of the work is the way it draws us into the world of Hosea to be addressed by Hosea's God. Sin is exposed not as breaking the law but rather breaking God's heart. Here we encounter the holy love of God, passionate, unchangeable and fiercely committed to turning a prostitute into a devoted wife. The prayer that accompanies this commentary is that it might stir our passion for God and his ways and to that we add our 'amen'.

Ken Armstrong
Pastor
Bessacarr Evangelical Church
Doncaster, England

HOSEA

The Passion of God

Tim Chester

CHRISTIAN
FOCUS

Tim Chester is an author, pastor of The Crowded House, Sheffield, and a leader of The Crowded House church planting network. He is married with two daughters.

Copyright © Tim Chester

ISBN 978-1-78191-368-0

10 9 8 7 6 5 4 3 2 1

Printed in 2014
by
Christian Focus Publications Ltd.,
Geanies House, Fearn, Ross-shire,
IV20 1TW, Scotland, UK.

www.christianfocus.com

Cover design by Daniel van Straaten

Printed and bound by
Bell & Bain, Glasgow

Contents

Introduction

In the message of Hosea we see the passion of God. We see the jealousy of God, the commitment of God, the heartbreak of God, the enthusiasm of God, the love of God. People often talk about what they feel about God. Hosea tells us what God feels about us.

So do not expect to discover what to do when your boss messes you around or when your child misbehaves or when you need to decide whether to move house. But do expect to discover the passion of God. It is, of course, important to apply the Bible to the details of our lives. But we need to do so in the light of the big picture. You can plan your daily routine. But what really sets the course of your life is your vision of God. The gospel is not a mechanical process with inputs and outputs. The gospel is relational. Hosea teaches us that it is deeply personal and heartfelt. It is reliable because the character of God Himself is reliable. We will see that, while God cannot be surprised, He can be disappointed. He cannot be thwarted, but He can be heartbroken.

It is my prayer that as we explore the message of Hosea the Spirit of God would so reveal God's passion that He stirs our passion: our jealousy for God, our commitment to God, our heartbreak at sin, our enthusiasm to serve, our love for the lost.

This is what we can expect from Hosea. We can expect God to expose our unfaithfulness and show us how fickle is our love (2:3). We can expect God to pursue us, wound us, rebuke us. In His passion for His glory and our good He will be ruthless. It will not always be comfortable. C. S. Lewis wrote:

> An 'impersonal God' – well and good. A subjective God of beauty, truth and goodness, inside our own heads – better still. A formless life-force surging through us, a vast power

which we can tap – best of all. But God himself, alive, pulling at the other end of the cord, perhaps approaching at an infinite speed, the hunter, king, husband – that's quite another matter.[1]

But we can also expect God to allure us, to embrace us, to speak tenderly to us (2:14). We can expect God to heal us and revive us, to bind our wounds and raise us up (6:1-2; 14:4). We can expect God to gather us beneath His shadow so that in the oppressive heat of life's problems we still flourish and blossom (14:5-7). We can expect God to come to us like rain on dry ground (6:3; 10:12). 'The LORD says, "Then I will heal you of your faithlessness; my love will know no bounds, for my anger will be gone forever. I will be to Israel like a refreshing dew from heaven"' (14:4-5, NTL).

Readers who want to get straight into the text may wish to skip this introductory material which covers the historical context of Hosea's ministry, the little we know about the man himself, his intended audience (or audiences), the text and structure of the book plus an overview of its key themes.

Historical Context
It is an age of great prosperity with new technologies. People are confident in the future. Faith is accepted, but only as long as it is restricted to our private religious lives. Public life carries on without much regard to God. Politics is full of intrigue and infighting. Foreign policy is dictated by national interests. Religious leaders hit the headlines because they have been caught in flagrant sin. The rich get richer while the poorer languish.

It sounds like a description of our context today. But it could also describe Hosea's context. The book of Hosea begins: 'The word of the LORD that came to Hosea son of Beeri during the reigns of Uzziah, Jotham, Ahaz and Hezekiah, kings of Judah, and during the reign of Jeroboam son of Jehoash king of Israel' (1:1). So Hosea ministered about two centuries after the division of God's people into two kingdoms. After the death of King Solomon, the ten northern tribes had formed the kingdom known as Israel or Ephraim and the two southern

---

1.   C. S. Lewis, *Miracles*, HarperCollins, 2001, p. 94.

tribes of Judah and Benjamin had formed the kingdom of Judah.

Hosea mentions four kings of Judah: Uzziah, Jotham, Ahaz and Hezekiah. Uzziah's (or 'Azariah' as he is also known) began reigning alongside his father in about 791 B.C. and Hezekiah died in 687/6. Together that is a period of over one hundred years! So it is likely Hosea started his ministry late in the reign in Uzziah in the south (whose reign ended in 740) and Jeroboam II in the north (whose reign ended in 753) and ended his ministry early in the reign of Hezekiah (who began reigning alongside is father in about 729). While Hosea predicts the disaster that is coming on the northern kingdom, he does not specifically mention the fall of Samaria in 722. This would suggest Hosea began his ministry at some point before 753 (when Jeroboam II died) and ended his ministry at some point between 729 and 722 (between Hezekiah's accession and the fall of Samaria). It may well be that the fall of Samaria was what brought his ministry to an end, perhaps because he was killed in the Assyrian invasion or carried into captivity or exiled in Judah. So Hosea was ministering over a 25-30-year period during the third quarter of the eighth century B.C. This means he was active at about the same time as the Prophets Isaiah, Amos and Micah.

Hosea's ministry began during a period of expansion and prosperity. The reigns of Uzziah in Judah and of Jeroboam II in Israel during the first half of the eighth century B.C. was the second golden age in the history of God's people (after the first golden age during the reigns of King David and King Solomon). The old enemy, the Arameans, were in a weakened position. The rising power of Assyria was still at this point preoccupied with its northern and eastern borders. So Israel did not feel any significant external pressures during this period.

As the prophet Amos also recognised, increased prosperity led to increased faithlessness among God's people. Hosea faced widespread Baal worship. The worship of Baal had first been introduced into Israel during the reign of King Ahab and his queen, Jezebel. Now it was back (2:7, 17; 11:2). People practised idolatrous worship on hilltops (4:13) and there were alternative centres of worship at Bethel and Gilgal

(9:15; 12:11). Their worship incorporated idolatrous images (8:5; 13:2; 14:8), sacred pillars (10:1-2), the consulting of spirits (4:12) and cultic prostitution (4:1-13; Amos 2:7-8).

There was also a growing abuse of power and privilege. VanGemeren describes it as 'a period of opulence, prosperity, opportunism, and scheming during which the rich and powerful availed themselves of all opportunities to live luxuriously. Hosea was God's messenger to a complacent, self-indulgent, and apostate people.'[2] Politicians and merchants in Samaria, Israel's capital, prospered while workers and farmers suffered. Hosea speaks of drunkenness, armed robbery and murder (7:1-7). There was widespread corruption among the leaders of the nation (4:1-2; 5:1-2; 6:6, 9; 7:1, 6-7). VanGemeren again:

> Israel has also become proud, and economic progress only added to its self-confidence. The social structure encouraged power, greed, self-indulgence, corruption of justice, luxurious living among the upper classes, and the decay of social unity. The affluent showed no sense of responsibility toward the poor. As the gap between the rich and the poor became ominously wide, the poor were reduced to the level of slaves while the aristocracy imitated royalty and adopted a lavish lifestyle.[3]

During this period Hosea's message must have sounded unlikely. He announced God's judgment in a time when all anyone could see was God's blessing.

But, after the death of Jeroboam II, the situation in the north began to unravel. Hosea begins by announcing the fall of the Jehu dynasty (1:4) and with its fall the internal political stability of Israel ended. Jeroboam II was followed by six kings in thirty years, three of whom ruled for less than two years each and four of whom were assassinated. One after another, kings seized the throne through military coups. The dagger ruled in Israel. Factions vied for control. Some favoured an alliance with Egypt, others favoured Assyria. None favoured the LORD. Assyria was resurgent and increasingly aggressive. The golden age of the first half of the eight century proved

---

2.   Willem A. VanGemeren, *Interpreting the Prophetic Word*, Zondervan, 1990, 105.

3.   Ibid.

merely a pause between Aramean aggression and Assyrian dominance. Eventually in 722, Assyria overwhelmed and destroyed the northern kingdom of Israel.

The run-up to this defeat provides the historical background to Hosea's prophecy. After the death of Jeroboam II, Tiglath-Pileser III of Assyria began making incursions to the west. The first was in 738 B.C. when he took Hamath. Rezin of Syria and Menahem of Israel tried to stave off further aggression by paying tribute (2 Kings 15:19-20). Menahem's son, Pekahiah, was assassinated by his army captain, Pekah, who then made himself king of Israel (2 Kings 15:23-25). Pekah formed an alliance with Rezin of Syria to try to escape the authority of Assyria. For this they wanted the help of Judah, but Ahaz king of Judah refused. So Israel and Syria joined together to fight against Judah to force Ahaz to join their anti-Assyrian coalition. This war is called the Syro-Ephraimite War (2 Kings 16:1-9; 2 Chron. 28:5-7; Isa. 7:1–8:22; Micah 7:7-20). Ahaz responded to this threat by calling on the help of Tiglath-Pileser III. The Assyrian king defeated the Syrians and destroyed their capital Damascus in 732 B.C. He then attacked Israel, carrying away a portion of the population into exile and appointing a pro-Assyrian king, Hoshea. But Hoshea then defied his Assyrian overlords by making an alliance with Egypt. Assyria under Shalmaneser V besieged Samaria before destroying the city and exiling her inhabitants in 722 B.C. This was the end of the ten northern tribes of Israel.

So Hosea ministers during the close of a period of prosperity and the beginning of a calamity that would eventually culminate in the end of the northern kingdom.

Audience

Nothing is known about Hosea the man outside of the book. He was probably from the northern kingdom since he describes the King of Israel as 'our king' (7:5). Linguistic scholars also believe Hosea's Hebrew reflects a northern dialect.

The message of Hosea is primarily addressed to the northern kingdom of Israel. There are, however, a number of references to the southern kingdom of Judah (1:7; 4:15; 5:1, 5, 8, 10, 12-14; 6:4; 8:14; 10:11; 12:2). In the past many critical scholars believed these reflected later Judean additions. But most recent scholarship accepts that Hosea was the primary author and believes the text is basically sound. Some of the references to Judah are clearly part of the poetic structure and could not be crude insertions made at some point after its original composition.

More significantly, there is every reason to suppose Hosea had a vision that embraced both kingdoms even if the focus of his own ministry was in the north. In 1:11, for example, he promises the reunification of Israel and Judah under one king: **And the children of Judah and the children of Israel shall be gathered together, and they shall appoint for themselves one head.** God's promises include a focus on the Davidic family and Jerusalem. A true prophet of God, even one ministering in the northern kingdom, could therefore not ignore God's purposes for the southern kingdom. The future of God's people was inevitably tied up with the Davidic dynasty that ruled in the south.

But there are indications that whoever compiled the book of Hosea in its canonical form added some editorial touches under the inspiration of the Holy Spirit. The opening verse (and possible the final verse) appears to be written by an editor and the same may be true of the third-person account of Hosea's marriage. Raymond Dillard and Tremper Longman say: 'It is not impossible that later faithful followers of the prophet's tradition saw the analogy between the situation in the south some decades after the prophet's death and made the connection by inserting Judean concerns into the text.'[4] Hosea's contemporary, the prophet Isaiah, had disciples and Hosea may have done so as well (Isa. 8:16). It is possible to imagine them as refugees from the northern kingdom carrying with them the words of Hosea and then compiling them in Judah where they also highlighted the resonances for the southern kingdom. Indeed it is possible that Hosea himself may have been involved in this process since we have no record of whether he survived the fall of Samaria or how he died. Willem VanGemeren concludes: 'After the fall of Samaria the godly community in Judah applied the prophetic message to themselves and preserved the prophetic tradition

---

4. Raymond B. Dillard and Tremper Longman III, *An Introduction to the Old Testament*, Apollos, 1995, 355.

in written form ... Hosea was God's prophets to Israel, who in his writing also spoke to Judah (1:7, 11; 4:15; 5:5, 10, 13; 6:4, 11: 11:12: 12:2) and still speaks to all who are grafted into the covenant grace.'[5]

We need to remember that the book of Hosea has two audiences in mind: the people who first *heard* Hosea's message as he proclaimed it and those who first *read* the written record of those oral messages. The first hearers were members of the northern kingdom. But, under the inspiration of the Holy Spirit, someone (and it could have been Hosea himself) gathered together his messages into a written form, believing that his message had continued relevance in the southern kingdom and beyond. This could have been Hosea himself, perhaps exiled in Judah after the fall of Samaria. But we know that a century later the prophet Jeremiah had a scribe who wrote down his words (Jer. 36, 45). Moreover, the opening chapter of Hosea is written as a third-person narrative. So there is no reason to reject the idea that Hosea had a Spirit-inspired compiler.

The opening verse lists four kings of Judah and only one king of Israel. Why list more southern kings when his ministry focused on the north? It may be because Jeroboam II in the north was followed by six kings in thirty years. So it would have been easier to correlate Hosea's ministry to the more stable situation in the southern kingdom. But it also reminds us that Hosea's first readers (as opposed to his first hearers) were in Judah. So it was natural for whoever compiled Hosea's messages to locate his ministry in relation to Judean kings.

Hosea ends: 'Who is wise? Let them realise these things. Who is discerning? Let them understand. The ways of the LORD are right; the righteous walk in them, but the rebellious stumble in them' (14:9). This seems to reflect the wisdom tradition in Israel. While other prophets draw on wisdom writings, it is unusual for the wisdom tradition to 'annotate', as it were, the final editing of a collection of prophetic oracles. It suggests that, whatever the original historical context, we are being invited to discern how the message applies to our generation. This requires wisdom. Analysis of the text is not enough. We also need to analyse our times. It is an invitation

---

5.   VanGemeren, *Interpreting the Prophetic Word*, 108-9.

to the kind of double listening to which John Stott calls us. Our job, says Stott, particularly of those who are preachers, is to bridge the apparent cultural chasm between the biblical world and the contemporary world. This requires what Stott calls 'double listening' — listening to the Word and to the world. Preachers should prepare their sermons with a Bible in one hand and a newspaper in the other.

> Double listening ... is the faculty of listening to two voices at the same time, the voice of God through Scripture and the voices of men and women around us. These voices will often contradict one another, but our purpose in listening to them both is to discover how they relate to each other. Double listening is indispensable to Christian discipleship and Christian mission.[6]

> It is only through the discipline of double listening that it is possible to become a 'contemporary Christian'. For then we see that the adjectives 'historical' and 'contemporary' are not incompatible, we learn to apply the Word to the world, and we proclaim good news which is both true and new. In sum, we live in the 'now' in the light of 'then'.[7]

> We must allow the word of God to confront us, to disturb our security, to undermine our complacency, and to overthrow our patterns of thoughts and behaviour.[8]

Text

There were, of course, no printed Bibles until the invention of the printing press in the fifteenth century. Before this, copies of the Bible had to be written out by hand. Inevitably a few mistakes crept in. (Printed Bibles can also include mistakes, most famously in the case of the so-called 'Wicked Bible' printing of the King James Version which left out the 'not' in Exodus 20 to create 'Thou shalt commit adultery'.) For the most part these variations are minor and they rarely affect significant matters of doctrine. Scholars are able to reconstruct the most likely original version using the many documents,

---

6.   John Stott, *The Contemporary Christian*, (IVP, 1992), 510

7.   Ibid., 363

8.   John Stott, *Culture and the Bible* (IVP, 1981), 33

fragments of documents and early translations of the Bible that survive. This important discipline is called textual criticism.

The text of Hosea is often thought to be one of the worst-preserved books in the Bible because many of the passages in it are hard to translate. People speculate that the circumstances in which it was brought to Judah from the northern kingdom of Israel after the collapse of that kingdom may have led to these problems. Where scholars have struggled to make sense of the Hebrew, they have often assumed the problem is caused by a transmission error. Many of them have then opted to resolve the issues by translating one of the early Greek, Syriac, Latin or Aramaic translations of the Old Testament (usually the Greek translation called the Septuagint) back into Hebrew and then use this reconstructed text as the basis for their English translation. The problem with this is you end up with an English version which is a translation (into English) of a translation (a reconstructed Hebrew text) of a translation (the Septuagint Greek translation) of the original Hebrew text.

Another explanation for the difficulties of translating the book of Hosea is that Hosea used a northern dialect of ancient Hebrew that is largely lost to us, dying with the death of the northern kingdom. Scholars disagree as to the extent to which the problems are caused by unreliable manuscripts and Hosea's northern dialect, though more recent commentators tend to place more store by the Hebrew versions we have.

The central message of Hosea is not much affected by these issues, but you will notice significant differences if you compare different English translations or look at their footnotes. Consider, for example, Hosea 4:4:

NIV: But let no one bring a charge, let no one accuse another, for your people are like those who bring charges against a priest.

ESV: Yet let no one contend, and let none accuse, for with you is my contention, O priest.

The numbering of verses in most English editions of the book differs from that in Hebrew editions. The final two verses in chapter 1 and the final verse in chapters 12 and 13 in English

Bibles are part of chapters 2, 13 and 14 respectively in the Hebrew Bible, with those chapters renumbered accordingly:

English Bibles	Hebrew Bible
1:10–2:21	2:1-25
11:12–12:14	12:1-15
13:16–14:9	14:1-10

Hosea uses more metaphor and word play than almost any other prophet. Israel is an unfaithful wife (1:2-9; 3:1-5: 9:1); disappearing morning mist (6:4); hot ovens (7:4-7); a silly dove (7:11); a faulty bow (7:16); a wild donkey (8:9); passing dew and chaff (13:3). God is a jealous husband (2:2-13); a frustrated shepherd (4:16); a destructive moth or undesired rot (5:12); a ferocious lion (5:14; 11:10; 13:7-8); and a trapper (7:12). God's coming judgment is like harvesting the whirlwind (8:7); the washing away of debris (10:7); the yoking of a recalcitrant heifer (10:11) and a return to wilderness (2:14). But God is also a forgiving husband (3:1-5); a healing physician (6:1-2); reviving rains (6:3); a loving parent (11:3-4); a protecting lion (11:10-11); a life-giving dew (14:5); and a fertile pine tree (14:8). This poetic panoply was perhaps required to give full expression to the passions of God that form Hosea's central theme.

Structure

There is no general agreement on the structure of the book of Hosea. The division between the story of Hosea's marriage in chapters 1–3 and the rest of the book 4–14 is clear. Most (though not all) commentators detect a transition between chapters 11 and 12, resulting in two cycles of judgment and hope (4–11 and 12–14). These may parallel the two cycles of hope in chapters 1–3 – judgment (1:2-9) and hope (1:10–2:1) and judgment (2:2-13) and hope (2:14–3:5). Certainly both 4:1 and 12:2 open in the courtroom:

- 'Hear the word of the LORD, you Israelites, because the LORD has a charge to bring against you who live in the land ...' (4:1)

- 'The LORD has a charge to bring against Judah ...' (12:2)

Both 5:8 and 8:1 begin with a call to sound the trumpet which suggests they may introduce new oracles.

Beyond this, the book contains few clear introductory phrases (like 'Thus says the Lord') or transition markers. Hosea begins: 'When the LORD began to speak through Hosea, the LORD said to him ...' (1:2) Thereafter it is assumed that what we are reading is the LORD's word given through the prophet. The phrase is not repeated to introduce new or separate messages. Brevard Childs concludes, 'the summary, compilatory nature of the present collection is only too obvious.'[9] Peter Craigie writes:

> It is as if the speeches of a contemporary politician, delivered over a lifetime in public service, were compiled into a single anthology; while each speech would have made perfect sense at the time and in the place where it was first delivered, each one would be more difficult to understand later when the specific occasion for the speech was forgotten. And so it is with Hosea; the substance of some of the speeches and sermons remains, but frequently the circumstances in which they were spoken can only be surmised.[10]

This said, two attempts to outline the structure of Hosea deserve mention.

Walter Kaiser argues that the threefold accusation in 4:1 shapes the rest of the book:[11] 'Hear the word of the LORD, O children of Israel, for the LORD has a controversy with the inhabitants of the land. There is no faithfulness or steadfast love, and no knowledge of God in the land.' These three charges – no faithfulness, no love and no knowledge – shape three cycles of judgment and promise in which each of these themes in turn is dominant. 'Each of these three charges was then taken up in reverse order, and each section closed with a bright picture of a better future day when God's love broke through the barriers of Israel's persistent sin.'[12]

---

9. Brevard S. Childs, *Introduction to the Old Testament as Scripture*, SCM, 1979, 378.

10. Peter Cragie, *Twelve Prophets Volume 1*, DSB, 1984, 6.

11. Walter C. Kaiser, Jr., *Toward an Old Testament Theology*, Zondervan, 1978, 199-200.

12. Ibid., 199.

1. No knowledge (4:1–6:3)

For example: 'My people are destroyed from lack of knowledge. Because you have rejected knowledge, I also reject you as my priests; because you have ignored the law of your God, I also will ignore your children.' (4:6)

2. No love (6:4–11:11)

For example: 'What can I do with you, Ephraim? What can I do with you, Judah? Your love is like the morning mist, like the early dew that disappears.' (6:4)

3. No faithfulness (11:12–14:9)

For example: 'Ephraim has surrounded me with lies, the house of Israel with deceit. And Judah is unruly against God, even against the faithful Holy One.' (11:12, NIV)

The problem with this proposal is that these three keywords appear too often elsewhere in the book to persuade us that this is the structure around which Hosea constructed his book. Furthermore, other words such as 'prostitution' or 'to prostitute' and 'return' also occur prominently throughout the book (fifteen times and twenty-three times respectively). But what Kaiser's proposal does highlight is the importance in Hosea of knowing God (in a relational sense), loving God (in a covenantal sense) and faithfulness to God (and the covenant).

Duane Garrett believes Hosea's structure derives from chapters 1–3.[13] He highlights two features of the opening chapters. First, chapter 1 is dominated by the account of Hosea's three children whose names represent both judgment and hope for God's people. Second, there are two versions of Hosea's marriage: a third-person account in chapter 1 and a first-person account in chapter 3. He further argues that chapter 2 is all part of the explanation of the name of Hosea's third child. Garrett then detects the same features in the remainder of the book. Groups of three, he claims, occur throughout chapters 4–7 starting with the threefold charge in 4:1. He argues that 4:1–5:15 builds on the three explanations of the names of Hosea's children. In chapters 8–14 the pattern

---

13. Duane A. Garrett, *Hosea, Joel*, NAC vol. 19a, B&H, 1997, 34-9.

switches from groups of three to 'antiphonal proclamations' in which the speaker moves back and forth between the LORD and the prophet. Just as we had a first-person and third-person account of Hosea's marriage, now we have a first-person (the LORD) and third-person (Hosea) accounts of God's relationship with His people.

Again, while the overall scheme does not persuade, the link between Hosea's marriage and God's marriage is clearly central and the idea of an antiphonal arrangement highlights the way this theme is developed in the book. Garrett concludes:

> Hosea's experience with the promiscuous Gomer has legitimated his call to be Yahweh's prophet ... What many would consider a disqualification for the office – a prophet whose own wife was morally out of control – serves in this case as his *credentials*. This is because Yahweh and Hosea have shared the same experience – that of marriage to an unfaithful spouse. Thus the book tells the stories of Hosea's and Yahweh's marriages in both first and third-person texts – each 'husband' speaks for himself and has the other speak on his behalf.[14]

Key Themes
Israel's disobedience manifests itself primarily in apostasy. The people have turned from God to idols (4:1-13; 5:11; 8:6; 13:2). The various forms of leadership in Israel are all complicit in leading the people astray: the priests (4:6; 5:1; 6:9; 10:5), the prophets (4:5), and the political rulers (5:1, 10; 7:3-7; 9:15). As a result the 'people are destroyed from lack of knowledge' (4:6). Their lack of trust in God has resulted in foreign alliances (5:13; 7:8-10; 8:9). So Hosea warns of coming judgment, a warning fulfilled in the Assyrian conquest of the northern kingdom and the Babylonian conquest of the southern kingdom. But there is also hope (11:8-9). God will heal the wounds of their disobedience and restore them in the land (14:1-9).

Spiritual adultery
Hosea was ministering around the same time as the prophet Amos and both announced God's judgment against the northern kingdom of Israel. But, whereas Amos focused on

---

14.   Garrett, *Hosea, Joel*, 36.

the social injustice of the nation, Hosea focuses on the spiritual infidelity of the nation. Amos declared that the people were unjust, Hosea that they were unfaithful. So Amos has been called 'the prophet of divine righteousness' while Hosea is 'the prophet of divine love'.[15] Hosea rarely uses the language of 'righteousness' and 'justice' and instead speaks of 'knowing God' and 'faithfulness'. Hosea uses God's personal, covenantal name 'Yahweh' (usually translated the LORD with capital letters in modern English translations) nearly twice as many times as he uses the generic term 'God' (Elohim).[16] And when Hosea does refer to 'God' (Elohim) it's usually with a personal pronoun ('Yahweh your God' in 12:9; 13:4; 14:1; 'your God' in 4:6; 9:1; 12:6; 'Yahweh their God' in 3:5; 7:10; 'their God' in 4:12; 5:4; 'my God' 2:23; 8:2; 9:17; 'our God' in 14:3; and 'her God' in 13:16).

Foundational for Hosea's message of spiritual infidelity is his own experience of marriage to an adulterous wife. Chapters 1 and 3 present us with an enacted parable. The adultery of Hosea's wife and her redemption enact the adultery of Israel and God's refusal to give her up. Chapter 2 provides a poignant commentary on this parable.

> God called Hosea not only to speak to the nation but also to serve as a living symbol of the larger spiritual reality of Yahweh's love for promiscuous Israel. By this means the truth of their violations of the covenant was made visibly literal before them. Such a bold demonstration was necessary because the people themselves could not see their departure from Yahweh: 'To me they cry, "My God, we Israel know you!" (Hosea 8:2).'[17]

Though most prominent in chapters 1–3, the theme of adultery continues beyond them. The words 'prostitution' or 'to prostitute' appear in a metaphorical sense fifteen times throughout the book, in addition to one reference to literal cultic prostitution (4:14). Chapter 4 opens in the divorce court with God making His charge against His people. Moreover, the

---

15.   Herman Veldkamp, *Hosea: Love's Complaint*, Paideia Press, 1980, 9.

16.   Hans Walter Wolff, *Hosea*, Hermeneia series, Fortress, 1965 ET 1974, xxv.

17.   Raymond C. Ortlund Jr., *God's Unfaithful Wife: A Biblical Theology of Spiritual Adultery*, NSBT Vol. 2, InterVarsity/Apollos, 1996, 47.

repeated word 'know' or 'acknowledge' is the same word as the word used in Genesis 4:1 to describe sexual intercourse, 'Now Adam *knew* Eve his wife, and she conceived and bore Cain ...' (ESV). Israel should have been a faithful wife who knew only her husband, but instead she has known other lovers.

The problem was not that the people were irreligious. The problem was not even that they had stopped worshipping Yahweh. The problem was their infidelity, their divided loyalties. 'As for my sacrificial offerings, they sacrifice meat and eat it, but the LORD does not accept them. Now he will remember their iniquity and punish their sins; they shall return to Egypt' (8:13). 'Israel was an unfaithful wife, sharing her love with both Yahweh and the Baals, and her lawful husband could no longer support her affairs with other lovers through further manifestations of his mercies.'[18]

Hosea employs daringly emotive language to speak of God's wounded jealously and enduring love. Commenting on Hosea 11:8-9, Walter Brueggemann says:

> It is as though YHWH, through the daring of the poet, reaches deeper into YHWH's own sensibility. There YHWH discovers, so the poet dares to say, a deep passion and, consequently, deep compassion for Israel that precludes the destruction just announced in verses 5-7. In this text the anticipated and legitimate punishment of Israel is foresworn; this divine resolve is different from and much more radical than 14:4-7, where healing comes after devastation. Here the devastation is averted. The ground for averted devastation, moreover, is YHWH's own sense of YHWH. YHWH is not 'a man' to react in anger; YHWH, rather, is 'God.' More than that, YHWH is 'the Holy One in Israel,' the God whose holy character is profoundly qualified by loyalty to Israel. This sense of self on YHWH's part is the ground for well-being in Israel, even when Israel's shabby treatment of YHWH merits otherwise.[19]

It was not only in the religious sphere, but also in the political arena that Israel was unfaithful. In moments of crisis she turned to other nations. 'For they have gone up to Assyria like a wild donkey wandering alone. Ephraim has sold herself

---

18. Ortlund, *God's Unfaithful Wife*, 47.

19. Walter Brueggemann, *An Introduction to the Old Testament: The Canon and Christian Imagination*, WJK, 2003, 218.

to lovers' (8:9). 'The spiritual answers and resources offered in the covenant seemed unreal in the face of visible dangers. Deuteronomic faith seemed irrelevant, and the God of the exodus and Sinai remote.'[20] 'Hosea knew what it was to preach to a sceptical crowd. With Assyrian war chariots parked on the border, and grown-up countries playing grown-up politics, the wisest course of action for Israel seems to have been to find the biggest friend in the school playground and join his gang.'[21]

> The people failed to make meaningful connections between their theology, history and worship, on the one hand, and their real-life problems, on the other hand. They put God, his covenant, his power, his wisdom, into a limiting category of thought – they could not bring themselves really to believe the assurance of Deuteronomy 28:1-14 – while 'the real world' was another category altogether with its own rules and its own resources. They acted as though faith in Yahweh alone were an impracticable policy for life, As a result, they dishonoured him even as they thought they continued to honour him.[22]

Children of God

The theme of God's people as God's bride is to the fore, but God's people as God's children is also a prominent theme:

> 'Yet the number of the children of Israel shall be like the sand of the sea, which cannot be measured or numbered. And in the place where it was said to them, "You are not my people," it shall be said to them, "Children of the living God"' (1:10).

> 'When Israel was a child, I loved him, and out of Egypt I called my son ... To them I was like one who lifts a little child to the cheek, and I bent down to feed them ... They will follow the LORD; he will roar like a lion. When he roars, his children will come trembling from the west' (Hosea 11:1, 4, 10, NIV).

Hosea 8:1; 9:4, 8, 15 speak of 'the house of the LORD', 'the house of his God' and 'my house'. The reference here is almost

20. Ortlund, *God's Unfaithful Wife*, 48.
21. Chris Green, 'Preaching in 3D,' *Commentary*, Oak Hill College, Winter 2010-2011, 19-21.
22. Ortlund, *God's Unfaithful Wife*, 48.

certainly to the household or family of God rather than to his temple (since there was no temple in in the northern kingdom of Israel).[23]

Sometimes the metaphors shift from husband/wife to father/children. But sometimes it is a development of the marriage metaphor: individual Israelites are the children born to collective Israel, bride and mother. Garrett says: 'Israel the wayward wife is the leadership, institutions, and culture of Israel. The children are the ordinary men and women who are trained and nurtured in that culture.'[24] So Garrett summarises the message of Hosea:

> Mother Israel is the shrines and sacrifices, the sacred blessings, the royal symbols and trappings, the armies, and the official teachings that are passed from generation to generation. Especially, Mother Israel is the priests and kings and other members of the ruling class who shape, direct, and exploit the people. Mother Israel is that which gives the people their identity. She is the institution that forms every Israelite generation.

> The children, again, are the common people. They are the farmers who want good crops, the mothers who want many children, and the common folk who want security and divine blessing. But something has gone terribly wrong. Mother Israel has abandoned Yahweh, her husband. She has embraced a new lover, Baal, because he claims to be able to enrich her with jewels and clothe her in the finest materials. She has also pursued other lovers-nations who can supposedly protect her and enrich her with trade. So enticed, Mother Israel has taught her children to serve Baal at the shrines. In doing this, she does not imagine that she has broken her marriage vows but supposes that she is faithful to the real meaning of those vows. Looking at the bulls of the shrines, she declares, 'These are your gods, who brought you out of Egypt!' (cf. Exod. 32:4).

> The children have followed their mother. Superstitious and fearful while at the same time captivated by that alluring benefit of Baalism, the cult prostitute, they know nothing of their father, Yahweh. Indeed, one cannot even say that Yahweh is their father. They are a lost generation, the children

---

23.   J. Andrew Dearman, *The Book of Hosea*, NICOT, 2010, 44-9.
24.   Garrett, *Hosea, Joel*, 39.

of Baal. They possess none of the three basic qualities that should mark the chosen people: integrity, compassion, and the knowledge of God. Their only hope of salvation is to turn from Mother Israel and go back to the one real Father, Yahweh. That is, to be true children of God they would have to abandon Mother Israel, for she is not his wife, and her children are Lo-Ammi, 'Not-my-people'. But this they cannot do. She has too well instructed them in her ways, and they belong to Baal. What shall Yahweh do with a people who can neither repent, nor even understand the need for it, nor recognise that Baal is a lie, nor divorce themselves from their mother and her ways? He must strip Mother Israel of all she has. That is, the institutions of Israel must die. The shrines must burn, the crops must fail, the kings and army must perish, the priests and princes must fall into disgrace, and Mother Israel and her children must once again wander in the wilderness. When this happens, at last, they will see both the truth and the lies for what they are and return to Yahweh, Husband and Father.[25]

Prosperity leads to self-reliance

Another theme is that the people misinterpret their prosperity. They regard it as a sign of Baal's blessing and a validation of the Baal fertility cult (2:8-9). This underlies their infidelity towards Yahweh. The tragic irony is that the blessing that arises from the LORD's commitment to His bride becomes the reason for her apostasy: 'When I fed them, they were satisfied; when they were satisfied, they became proud; then they forgot me' (13:6). 'At issue was the all-sufficiency of Yahweh, with the question perhaps put this way: Where does life, in all its richness and fulness, come from? Does it come from Yahweh alone, or from Yahweh plus others?'[26]

One striking feature of Hosea's treatment of this theme is the way he *reinterprets* the language of Baal worship. He takes the language of Canaanite syncretism, especially the idea of divine-human marriage, and reapplies it to Yahweh, the God of Israel's history. In so doing, he subverts the language.

Yahweh, not Baal, was the Lord of the land, who was Israel's faithful lover and forgotten provider of bounty. Hosea

25.   Garrett, *Hosea, Joel*, 39-40.
26.   Ortlund, *God's Unfaithful Wife*, 49.

confronted the mythological concepts of Canaanite religion with a 'realistic' language which laid claim to all areas of life in the name of Yahweh ... Hosea's use of language was 'realistic', that is, it opposed the Canaanite mythological concept of deity and land with a theological alternative: Yahweh was Israel's 'lord' (Baal) and lover. Hosea chose to stand within the mythological world-view and shatter it by introducing a new referent for the old language.[27]

In other words, Hosea uses the language of the Baal fertility cult (especially in chapter 2), but uses it to describe Yahweh's covenantal care of His people. Israel looked to the fertility religion of Baal to provide, but God Himself is their provider (2:5-13). Today, perhaps, it is Tesco and Walmart. It is the god of the market to whom we look to be our provider, our Jehovah Jireh, and whose laws we obey.

Living in the story
Hosea is full of references to Israel's history, from recent events back to its prehistory in the story of the patriarchs. Working back, Hosea alludes to:

- the assassinations and coups of the past decade (7:7; 8:4)

- the crimes of the Jehu dynasty in 844 B.C. (1:4)

- the early monarchy (9:15; 13:10-11)

- the early turning of Israel to Baal worship (9:10)

- the gift of the Promised Land (2:8, 15; 9:10)

- the wilderness wanderings (2:3, 14; 9:10; 12:13; 13:5)

- the exodus from slavery in Egypt (2:15; 11:1; 12:13; 13:4)

- the story of Jacob (12:2-6, 12)

- the destruction of Admah and Zeboiim with Sodom and Gomorrah (11:8; see Deut. 29:23)

- the promise to Abraham (1:10)

- the sin of Adam (6:7)

---

27.   Childs, *Introduction to the Old Testament as Scripture*, 378-9.

Sometimes this history is told to accentuate the horror of Israel's infidelity to a God who has been so good to her over so many years. Sometimes Hosea sees the story being replayed. Sometimes this is for ill as, for example, Israel turns again to the Baals as she did when she first entered the land of Canaan (9:10). It seems that whether it is the beginning of the Jehu dynasty (1:4) or the monarchy (9:15; 13:10-11) or entry into the Promised Land (9:10) infidelity is always present. 'Wherever Israel's beginnings are examined, her present immediately appears; indeed, the present is the end of the earlier beginnings of that history.'[28] As a result, it seems the story will go into reverse. In judgment Israel's history will rewind and she will return to the wilderness or to Egypt (ch. 9). But sometimes hope, too, is found in the replaying of the story. God will again woo His people as He did in their origins and again lead them out of wilderness (2:14-15). Von Rad concludes:

> Hosea's whole preaching is rooted in the saving history. It might almost be said that he only feels safe when he can base his arguments in history. Jahweh is Israel's God 'from the land of Egypt' (Hosea 12:9; 13:4); by the prophet Moses, Jahweh brought Israel up from Egypt (Hosea 12:13). This early history of Israel was the time when Jahweh was able to give her his entire love (Hosea 11:4).[29]

Douglas Stuart argues that central to Hosea's message is the outworking of the blessings and curses in Deuteronomy.

> Understanding the message of the book of Hosea depends upon understanding the Sinai covenant. The book contains a series of blessings and curses announced for Israel by God through Hosea. Each blessing or curse is based upon a corresponding type in the Mosaic law. Some blessings and curses so specifically parallel the pentateuchal formulations that they border on 'citation' ... Hosea's task was simply to warn that Yahweh intended to enforce the terms of his covenant.[30]

---

28. Wolff, *Hosea*, xxvii.

29. Gerhard von Rad, *Old Testament Theology Volume II*, Oliver and Boyd, 1960 ET 1965, 140.

30. Douglas Stuart, *Hosea-Jonah*, WB.C. 31, Word, 1987, 6-7.

Israel experiences judgment because she has broken the covenant (6:7; 8:1) – the covenant break symbolised by Hosea's broken marriage covenant (1–3). The story Hosea tells conforms to that predicted by Moses in Deuteronomy 4:25-31 – a story of idolatry leading to exile, but also of return because of God's mercy.

Turning
The word 'turn' or 'return' or 'repent' is used twenty-two times in Hosea in varied and contrasting ways. It is hard to avoid the idea that Hosea is intentionally playing on these varied associations. It is used to denote:

Repentance:

- in descriptions of Israel's repentance (2:7; 3:5)

- in calls on Israel to repent (6:1; 12:6; 14:1-2)

- in descriptions of Israel's failure to repent (5:4; 7:10, 16; 11:5b)

Judgment:

- in the sense of God turning back His blessing (2:9; 5:15; 6:11)

- in the sense of God returning or repaying Israel's deeds (4:9; 12:2, 14)

- in the sense of God returning Israel to Egypt (8:13; 9:3; 11:5a)

Salvation:

- in the sense of God not turning to judgment (11:9)

- in the sense of God turning away His anger (14:4)

- in the sense of God returning Israel to a blessed state (14:7 which is literally '[Israel] will return to flourishing like the grain')

Two examples are particularly striking. In Hosea 11:5, we read: 'Will they not *return* to Egypt and will not Assyria rule over them because they refuse to *repent*?' Because the people refuse to return, they will be forced to return – to return to Egypt. The second example is in the song of Hosea 14 which is divided into two halves: a liturgy of repentance and a song of God's restoration. Both begin with 'turning'. We turn to God in repentance and He responds by turning away his anger.

> *Return*, O Israel, to the LORD your God,
> for you have stumbled because of your iniquity.
> Take with you words and *return* to the LORD ...
> I will heal their apostasy; I will love them freely,
> for my anger has *turned* from them. (14:1-4)

Divine sovereignty and judgment
Commenting on 8:4 ('They made kings, but not through me. They set up princes, but I knew it not'), von Rad says:

> While the people still believed that in these coronations in Samaria they could see Jahweh in action as the protector of his people, Hosea recognised precisely in these political events that Jahweh's judgment upon Israel was already in full sweep. 'I give you a king in my anger and take him away in my wrath' (Hosea 13:11). This is, in fact, quite one of the most essential elements in Hosea's view – while his fellows eagerly strive to repair the ravages in the state of affairs, and to guard themselves against threats by taking political measures, Hosea sees that the root of the trouble goes much deeper. It is God himself who has turned against them; the nation is suffering from God, who is seated like an ulcer in its belly.[31]

Chris Green says: 'Hosea is insistent that God is no stranger to the rough and tumble either of international diplomacy or the pettiness of domestic politics (see Hosea ch. 5 throughout). God is a real and living God, who is not being left behind by tomorrow's headlines.'[32]

The Use of Hosea in the New Testament
A number of phrases from Hosea are echoed in the New Testament. Hosea 6:6 ('mercy not sacrifice'), especially as it reads in the LXX, is echoed in Matthew 9:13 and 12:7. Hosea 10:8 (the reference to people calling on rocks to cover them) is echoed

---

31. von Rad, *Old Testament Theology*, 143.
32. Green, 'Preaching in 3D,' 19-21.

in Luke 23:30 and Revelation 9:16. Hosea 10:12 ('a harvest of righteousness') is echoed in 2 Corinthians 9:10. Hosea 14:2 ('the fruit of our lips') is echoed in Hebrews 13:15. Hosea 12:8 ('I am rich, I have prospered') is echoed in Revelation 3:17.

'Then the LORD said, "Call him Lo-Ammi (which means 'not my people'), for you are not my people, and I am not your God"' (1:9) and 'I will show my love to the one I called "Not my loved one". I will say to those called "Not my people", "You are my people"; and they will say, "You are my God"' (2:23) are cited in Romans 9:25 to support the inclusion of the Gentiles in the purposes of God and in 1 Peter 2:10 to describe the identity of Jews and Gentiles together as God's people.

'I will deliver this people from the power of the grave; I will redeem them from death. Where, O death, are your plagues? Where, O grave, is your destruction? I will have no compassion' (13:14) is cited in 1 Corinthians 15:55 to celebrate the defeat of death through the cross.

'When Israel was a child, I loved him, and out of Egypt I called my son (11:1) is used in Matthew 2:15 as a prophecy of the return of Jesus from His period as a refugee in Egypt, suggesting Jesus personifies the people of God and recapitulates their story.

We will explore the significance of these allusions further as we meet them in the text.

Commentaries

I have kept interaction and quotations from other commentaries to a minimum. But the following commentaries were my companions during my time with Hosea.

Elizabeth Achtemeier (1996), *Minor Prophets I*, New International Biblical Commentary, Henderson.

Francis I. Andersen and David Noel Freedman (1980), *Hosea*, Anchor Bible, Doubleday.

John Calvin (1989), *Commentaries on the Twelve Minor Prophets, Vol. 1, Hosea* in *Calvin's Commentaries, Vol. XIII*, Baker.

Peter Craigie (1984), *The Twelve Prophets Volume I*, The Daily Study Bible series, Saint Andrew Press/Westminster Press.

J. Andrew Dearman (2010), *The Book of Hosea*, New International Commentary on the Old Testament, Eerdmans.

Michael Eaton (1996), *Hosea*, Christian Focus.

Duane A. Garrett (1997), *Hosea, Joel*, New American Commentary vol. 19a, B&H.

David Allan Hubbard (1989), *Hosea*, Tyndale Old Testament Commentary, IVP.

Derek Kidner (1981), *The Message of Hosea*, Bible Speaks Today, IVP.

John L. MacKay (2012), *Hosea*, Mentor.

James Luther Mays (1969), *Hosea*, Old Testament Library, SCM.

Thomas Edward McComiskey (1992), 'Hosea' in *The Minor Prophets: An Exegetical and Expository Commentary Volume 1*, ed. Thomas Edward McComiskey, Baker.

Henry McKeating (1971), *Amos, Hosea, Micah*, The Cambridge Bible Commentary, CUP.

Gary V. Smith (2001), *Hosea, Amos, Micah*, NIV Application Commentary, Zondervan.

Douglas Stuart (1987), *Hosea-Jonah*, Word Biblical Commentary, Word.

Herman Veldkamp (1980), *Hosea: Love's Complaint*, trans. Theodore Plantinga, Paideia Press.

Hans Walter Wolff (1965 ET 1974), *Hosea*, Hermeneia series, trans. Gary Stansell, Fortress.

1

God Promises A People
(Hosea 1:1–2:1)

Let me tell you a story. It is a story that begins with the beginning of time when God first made the world. It was a beautiful world, a perfect world. God placed humanity in His world to be His people, to know Him and enjoy Him, to love Him and to be loved by Him, to be His people and to be their God.

But we rejected God's love. We were unfaithful to Him. We walked away from the relationship. As a result, the world was cursed and humanity came under God's judgment. We made a mess of our relationship with God and our relationships with one another.

But God began a plan to create a renewed world with a renewed people. He came to a man called Abram and promised that he would become a people, a people who were blessed by God. God changed his name to Abraham, which means 'father of many'. God promised that Abraham's family would be like the sand on the seashore that cannot be counted.

And this is what happened. Abraham's family became a nation. Abraham had a son called Isaac, and Isaac had a son called Jacob, and Jacob had twelve sons, and their descendants became a nation. God gave Jacob a new name, Israel, and so this nation was called Israel. It had twelve tribes, each descended from one of the sons of Jacob.

To escape a famine, Jacob's family ended up in Egypt. It was in Egypt that this family became a nation. At first they were welcomed in Egypt, but over time they became enslaved. They cried out and God had mercy on them. He rescued them from Egypt by His power through a man called Moses. Through Moses, God told the Israelites, 'You will be my people and I will be your God.'

God gave to Israel the land of Canaan, the land that today we call Palestine. Their greatest king was David, who gave the people peace and prosperity. His son Solomon was famous for his wisdom. But he also married foreign wives and followed foreign gods. Solomon enslaved God's people all over again to force them to work on his building projects.

Solomon was succeeded by his son Rehoboam. Rehoboam extended Solomon's slave labour programme. This precipitated a rebellion under the leadership of a man named Jeroboam. In 930 B.C. the twelve tribes of Israel divided into two kingdoms. The ten northern tribes formed a separate nation under Jeroboam I while the two southern tribes of Judah and Benjamin remained under the rule of David's dynasty. During the time of this division the ten northern tribes were called 'Israel' or sometimes 'Ephraim' (after the largest tribe) and its capital was Samaria. The two southern tribes were called 'Judah' after their larger tribe and their capital was Jerusalem.

Jeroboam got the new northern nation of Israel off to a bad start. He did not want his people travelling to the temple in Jerusalem and being subject to the propaganda of Judah. So he erected two golden calves, one at Dan in the north of his kingdom and one at Bethel in the south. He made these self-invented idols the focus of Israelite worship.

The southern kingdom of Judah continued to be ruled over by the family of David. But in the northern kingdom of Israel there were a succession of coups. The five kings after Jeroboam all came to power through bloodshed (Nadab, Baasha, Elah, Zimri, Tibni). None of them did anything to stop the idolatry in the kingdom. Eventually Omri established a dynasty. He became king in 880 B.C. after five years of civil war. But his dynasty was cruel and wicked. He was succeeded by his son Ahab. One of Ahab's palaces was in a town called Jezreel. It was there, when he wanted to appropriate a local vineyard, that Ahab had its owner Naboth falsely accused and murdered. This act became the epitome of the abuse of power in Israel's history (1 Kings 21).

Ahab's wife was Jezebel, whose name is synonymous with idolatry and spiritual adultery. Together they effectively made Baal worship the state religion in the northern kingdom. Baal, which means 'lord' or 'master' (Hosea 2:16-17), was the god of the Canaanites. He took many forms, so is sometimes spoken of as plural (Baals or Baalim). Baal worship was a fertility religion. This move towards Baal worship was opposed by the prophets Elijah and Elisha.

Ahab was succeeded by his children Ahaziah and Joram. But God raised up an army officer called Jehu to bring down the house of Omri. Jehu took power through great bloodshed. At their palace in Jezreel, Jehu slaughtered the leading figures in Ahab's family and then had the severed heads of all seventy of his grandsons brought to Jezreel. So Jezreel became synonymous with bloodshed (2 Kings 9–10).

Jehu was succeeded by son, grandson and great-grandson – Jehoahaz, Jehoash and Jeroboam II – so that four generations of Jehu's family ruled over Israel. But Jehu's family were little better than Omri and Ahab. Jehu removed Baal worship, but replaced it with other forms of idolatry. And in time the fertility cult of Baal made a comeback on an even bigger scale.

Jehu's great-grandson, Jeroboam II, ruled for over forty years. His reign was a reign of prosperity and peace. It was something of a golden age, second only to the era of David and Solomon. Everything looked rosy.

But then one day God called a man named Hosea, a man no one had heard of before.

> The word of the LORD that came to Hosea, the son of Beeri, in the days of Uzziah, Jotham, Ahaz, and Hezekiah, kings of Judah, and in the days of Jeroboam the son of Joash, king of Israel. (1:1)

This is the political context in which God called Hosea as a prophet: a time of prosperity that had led to spiritual complacency, a time of spiritual complacency that had led to spiritual infidelity. It was a time that was coming to a close.

Already the empire of Assyria was growing in power. A threat was building in the north.

A wife of whoredom (1:2)

But the real problem was not the political power of Assyria. The real problem was the spiritual state of Israel. The real threat was the judgment of God.

> When the LORD first spoke through Hosea, the LORD said to Hosea, 'Go, take to yourself a wife of whoredom and have children of whoredom, for the land commits great whoredom by forsaking the LORD.' (1:2)

'Whoredom', 'whoredom', 'whoredom'. Three times the LORD uses the word so that we cannot escape its impact. This was God's explanation: **'like an adulterous wife this land is guilty of unfaithfulness to the LORD'** (1:2, NIV). We can often approach a prophetic book like Hosea with a lack of enthusiasm, even with embarrassment. We know we are going to read about judgment and that does not go down well in our generation. But *we are Gomer*, Hosea's wife. We are adulterous, guilty of unfaithfulness. In response to God's love, kindness and patience, we have prostituted ourselves to other things. We have sold ourselves to other gods and got nothing in return but misery and threat. That is what sin is.

A child called Bloodshed (1:3-5)

Verse 2 says **Go, take** and in verse 3 we read **He went and took**. Hosea's obedience is immediate and complete – despite the pain he undoubtedly realised his obedience would involve.

> So he went and took Gomer, the daughter of Diblaim, and she conceived and bore him a son. (1:3)

She conceived and bore him a son suggests the first child was Hosea's. The other two children are introduced in a more ambiguous way: **Gomer conceived again and gave birth to a daughter ... Gomer had another son ...** (6, 8). Hosea is not mentioned. Maybe they are not his children. Maybe they are **children of whoredom** (2). It is not possible to be sure.

And the LORD said to him, 'Call his name Jezreel, for in just a little while I will punish the house of Jehu for the blood of Jezreel, and I will put an end to the kingdom of the house of Israel. And on that day I will break the bow of Israel in the Valley of Jezreel.' (1:4-5)

Hosea and Gomer had a son and God told them to call him **Jezreel**. God explains, **I will bring the bloodshed of Jezreel upon the house of Jehu.**

Jezreel was the name of the vineyard owned by Naboth and stolen by King Ahab. The problem is that God now pronounces judgment on the house of Jehu, not the house of Ahab. And Jehu was the man whom God used to judge Ahab. It is likely that **the house of Jehu** in verse 4 represents the house of Israel as a whole. But if the crime was Ahab's, why not use the house of Ahab to represent Israel rather than the man who deposed him? So the reference to Jezreel must be more than a reference to the crime of Ahab.

Jezreel was also the place where Jehu had massacred the family of Ahab when he took power. Is this what God has in mind? The problem is that Jehu replaced Ahab at God's behest. It could be that Jehu's house is judged because, even though he defeated Ahab as God commanded, he did so with excessive cruelty. Perhaps, but the Bible does not say this. Indeed at the time God commended Jehu: 'Because you have done well in carrying out what is right in my eyes, and have done to the house of Ahab according to all that was in my heart, your sons of the fourth generation shall sit on the throne of Israel' (2 Kings 10:30).

It is true, however, that God ordered Jehu to defeat Ahab to re-establish pure religion in Israel. Yet, although initially Jehu opposed Baal worship (2 Kings 10:18-28), he turned out to be just as bad (2 Kings 10:29-31). The bloodshed of Ahab was therefore in vain. It did not lead to Israel being purged of idolatry. So outwardly Jehu did as he was ordered. But inwardly he did it for his glory. His self-confessed passion for the LORD was not genuine, nor was it sustained. He allowed pagan religion to return.

But perhaps the point is simply that the word **Jezreel** had become a byword for bloodshed. God is saying that He will bring the kind of bloodshed for which Jezreel is known not just on the house of Ahab, but on the house of Israel as a whole.

On 8 August 1974, President Nixon resigned after the Watergate scandal. Members of his Republican Party election campaign team had been found guilty of breaking into the offices of the opposing Democratic Party in the Watergate office complex. As evidence of his complicity grew, Nixon was forced to resign. Watergate became the archetypal political scandal. As a result, the suffix '-gate' is routinely appended to words to denote some new scandal.

It seems the same thing happened to the word **Jezreel**. It has become the epitome of bloodshed. What Jehu did to the house of Ahab will now happen to his own house because of his (later) sins.

To us, **Jezreel** just sounds like a strange foreign name. But to Hosea it meant 'Bloodshed'. It was like calling a child 'Auschwitz' or 'Hiroshima' or 'Dunblane'. 'Here's my son; he's called Bloodshed.' 'Oh, I can't come today, I'm spending time with Bloodshed.'

It is not just the family of Jehu who will be judged. The whole political entity of Israel will be brought down. **And on that day I will break the bow of Israel in the Valley of Jezreel** (1:5). A bow was a symbol of military strength (Gen. 49:24; 1 Sam. 2:4; 2 Sam. 1:18; 2 Kings 13:15-16; Ps. 7:12; Ezek. 39:3). So breaking the bow is usually a metaphor for God's protection against the bows of Israel's enemies. Psalm 46:9 says: 'He makes wars cease to the end of the earth; he breaks the bow and shatters the spear; he burns the chariots with fire.' In Hosea 2:18 God promises: 'I will abolish the bow, the sword, and war from the land, and I will make you lie down in safety.' In these contexts, abolishing the bow is synonymous with safety. But here in 1:5 it is not the bow of Israel's enemies that will be destroyed. Instead it is the bow of Israel herself. She will be left defenceless. The Valley of Jezreel had once been the site of Gideon's victories (Judg. 6:33). Now it will be the place of Israel's fall. God was saying in effect: 'I'm going to destroy the political system of Israel and break its military power in the Valley of Jezreel.'

It is actually a pun. 'Jezreel' sounds like 'Israel' – even in English. 'You're not Israel, you're Jezreel, you're Bloodshed.'

It is akin to saying, 'You're not an evangelical church, but un-angelic church' or 'You're not a Reformed church, but a Deformed church'.

A child called Unloved (1:6-7)

Hosea and Gomer had a second child and God told them to call it, **Lo-Ruhamah**, which means 'Unloved'.

> She conceived again and bore a daughter. And the LORD said to him, 'Call her name No Mercy, for I will no more have mercy on the house of Israel, to forgive them at all. But I will have mercy on the house of Judah, and I will save them by the LORD their God. I will not save them by bow or by sword or by war or by horses or by horsemen.' (1:6-7)

Imagine how this worked out in the playground. 'There's Unloved.' 'See that child, she's Unloved.' A beautiful little girl called Unloved. A beautiful little girl with a forlorn look in her eyes. Every time someone calls her name they declare that she is Unloved.

The word literally means 'no compassion' or 'no mercy'. God will have no more mercy on Israel. It is an expression of the power of God's opposition to spiritual adultery. In His jealousy He withholds His mercy. Listen to Calvin's prayer in response to these verses:

> Grant, Almighty God, that as we were from our beginning lost, when thou wert pleased to extend to us thy hand, and to restore us to salvation for the sake of thy Son; and that as we continue even daily to run headlong to our own ruin, — O grant that we may not, by sinning so often, so provoke at length thy displeasure as to cause thee to take away from us the mercy which thou hast hitherto exercised towards us, and through which thou hast adopted us: but by thy Spirit destroy the wickedness of our heart, and restore us to a sound mind, that we may ever cleave to thee with a true and sincere heart, that being fortified by thy defence, we may continue safe even amidst all kinds of danger, until at length thou gatherest us into that blessed rest, which has been prepared for us in heaven by our Lord Jesus Christ. Amen.[1]

---

1.   John Calvin, *Commentaries on the Twelve Minor Prophets, Vol. 1, Hosea*, in *Calvin's Commentaries, Vol. XIII*, Baker, 1989, 60.

The southern kingdom of Judah is different. **Yet I will show love to Judah,' said God, 'and I will save them – not by bow, sword or battle, or by horses and horsemen, but I, the LORD their God, will save them'** (1:7, NIV). In verse 5, the bow cannot save Israel because God will break the bow. In verse 7, the bow cannot save Judah (nor any other piece of military kit). But God can save them. What matters is not our military hardware, but the mercy of God. What protects us is not our power or our wealth or our abilities, but the mercy of God.

In fact, God's judgment against Israel may be more ambiguous. Verse 6 literally reads, **For I will no more have mercy on the house of Israel, and I shall completely forgive them**. This appears to make no sense. How can God both show no mercy on Israel and also completely forgive Israel? Commentators get round this either by making the negative that begins the sentence control both clauses (hence the translations of ESV and NIV) or they argue that the word for forgiveness can also mean 'lift', giving the sense, 'I will no more have mercy on the house of Israel, but I will take them away' (into exile).[2] Garrett, however, wants to retain the sense of completely forgive even though it is 'jolting'.[3] It is a hint perhaps that God's people might have a future beyond judgment. A moment will come when God will both execute judgment without mercy and offer mercy without judgment. That moment is the cross. At the cross Jesus experiences the full wrath of God. As a result, His people are forgiven.

A child called Not My People (1:8-9)

> When she had weaned No Mercy, she conceived and bore a son. And the LORD said, 'Call his name Not My People, for you are not my people, and I am not your God.'

Hosea and Gomer had a third child, a son. God told them to call him, **Lo-Ammi** which means 'Not My People'. Hosea walked out to show his new son to his neighbours, friends and relatives and, holding the baby in his arms, said, 'This

2.   Thomas Edward McComiskey, 'Hosea' in *The Minor Prophets: An Exegetical and Expository Commentary Vol. 1*, ed. Thomas Edward McComiskey, Baker, 1992, 24-5.

3.   Garrett, *Hosea, Joel*, 60-1.

is Not-My-Boy'. He would stand in the street and say, 'See that child over there, he's Not-My-Son.' If Lo-Ruhamah found it difficult in the playground, imagine what it felt like to be called Not-My-Boy!

God told Hosea to call him Lo-Ammi because **You are not my people and I am not your God**. This is not what God had promised to Moses all those years before: 'You shall be my people and I shall be your God' (Exod. 6:7). In Leviticus 26:12, God had promised: 'I will walk among you and will be your God, and you shall be my people.' This is the promise or refrain at the heart of the Bible story. (See Jer. 24:7; 30:22; 31:33; 32:38; Ezek. 36:28; Hosea 2:23; Rev. 21:3-4.)

But not any more, not for the people of Israel. Now the promise goes into reverse. **You are *not* my people and I am *not* your God**. The great I AM who had covenanted to be *with* His people and *for* His people will no longer be with them or for them. The LORD whose presence marked them out as His special people abandons His people, leaving them as a pagan nation. They are alone with a superpower army bearing down on them. Imagine a child out walking with her father and they are approached by an angry dog. Imagine her turning round to find her father has gone. Imagine him saying as he runs away, 'You're not my child and I'm not your father.'

This is what happened. A few years later, the Assyrian army came crashing down on the kingdom of Israel and wiped it off the map. Israel was removed from the pages of history. The capital of Samaria was completely destroyed. The nation disappeared. All that remained were a few people mixed with other nations practising a half-remembered syncretistic version of their religion – the people who would later be called the Samaritans.

Why the weird names? Why blight the lives of these children in this way? Because God wanted to shake His people out of their infidelity before it was too late. He could have come without warning. Or He could have made do with Hosea preaching sermons. But He went further. He embodied His message in the names of Hosea's family to convey, then and now, His call to return before it is too late. 'In the marriage from which the children came, the guilt of faithless Israel lived before his very eyes. The children with these peculiar names forced the people to hear the word of Yahweh, since they raised questions, that elicited from the prophet again and again (vv. 4 and 5) those words which had been divinely entrusted to him.'[4]

The story continues (1:10–2:1)

Was this the end of the promise? Was this the end of God's plan of salvation? Was this the end of the story? No, God keeps His promises. God does not give up on His plans. God said to Hosea:

> Yet the number of the children of Israel shall be like the sand of the sea, which cannot be measured or numbered. And in the place where it was said to them, 'You are not my people,' it shall be said to them, 'Children of the living God.' And the children of Judah and the children of Israel shall be gathered together, and they shall appoint for themselves one head. And they shall go up from the land, for great shall be the day of Jezreel. Say to your brothers, 'You are my people,' and to your sisters, 'You have received mercy.'

God promises:

1. A restoration of the people

The number of the children of Israel shall be like the sand of the sea, which cannot be measured or numbered. God had promised the Patriarchs: 'I will make your offspring like the dust of the earth, so that if anyone could count the dust, then your offspring could be counted' (Gen. 13:16; see also 15:5; 22:17). That promise was threatened by the impending judgment of God. God's people were facing destruction and deportation. Isaiah had said: 'For though your people Israel be as the sand of the sea, only a remnant of them will return. Destruction is decreed, overflowing with righteousness' (Isa. 10:22). But Hosea echoes the promise to Abraham. Hosea's generation might be wiped out, but a remnant will remain and from this remnant God will restore His people.

2. A renewal of the covenant

And in the place where it was said to them, "You are not my people," it shall be said to them, "Children of the

---

4.   Wolff, *Hosea*, 22.

living God." As we have seen, God was about to repudiate His people in His judgment (1:9). But now Hosea promises a renewal of the covenant relationship. The refrain that had echoed down Israel's history would be heard again.

3. A reconciliation of the divisions

And the children of Judah and the children of Israel shall be gathered together. From the time of King Rehoboam, the son of Solomon, the nation had been divided into the northern kingdom of Israel and the southern kingdom of Judah. Throughout this period of division they were often at war. Throughout this time, God's promise to have a people who would be His people continually begged the question, Which people? Which nation? But now God promises to gather them together and re-form them as one nation.

4. A reinstatement of the king

And they shall appoint for themselves one head. One nation would require one king. The family of David would again rule over a united nation (see Ezekiel 37:15-28).

5. A return to the land

And they shall go up from the land, for great shall be the day of Jezreel (1:11). The people of God will be restored in the land. **Jezreel** does not literally mean 'bloodshed'. It came to be synonymous with bloodshed, but that was not its original meaning. Its original meaning is 'God plants'. Now Jezreel will no longer be synonymous with bloodshed. It will revert to its true meaning. God will plant His people in the land and they will flourish, they will be fruitful. The NLT translates this verse, **What a day that will be – the day of Jezreel – when God will again plant his people in his land.** The people will spring up from the land like vegetation because Jezreel will become an abundant harvest field. So at the end of chapter 2 we read:

> '"In that day, I will answer,"
>   says the LORD.
> I will answer the sky as it pleads for clouds.
> And the sky will answer the earth with rain.
> Then the earth will answer the thirsty cries

of the grain, the grapevines, and the olive trees.
And they in turn will answer,
"Jezreel" – "God plants!"' (2:21-22, NLT)

6. A recognition of God

There is perhaps one more element at which Hosea hints. Hosea describes God as **the living God** in verse 10. It was hardly news that God is alive. But the point is clear. The LORD, the God of Israel, is the living God in contrast to the dead gods of Canaan with whom Israel has been prostituting herself. Israel would come to recognise that their idols are impotent and imaginary. Only the LORD was the living God.

A faithful few would survive the judgment of God. The story would go on and the promise would be handed down from generation to generation. So it would continue until 750 years later, when the faithful few came down to just one person, Jesus Christ. The time would come when there was just one faithful Israelite. And He hung on a tree outside Jerusalem. He bore the rejection of God's people, the judgment of our sin and died our death. And then there was no one left. God's faithful people were no more.

But on the third day He rose again. And so there is a new people of God. God's people are resurrected. All who align themselves to Christ by faith, all who belong to Him, are God's faithful people. And His new life is our new life. At the cross God's jealous anger and passionate love came together: God judged Christ for our adultery so that we can again be His family.

Later on, Hosea says: 'Come, let us return to the LORD. He has torn us to pieces but he will heal us; he has injured us but he will bind up our wounds. After two days he will revive us; on the third day he will restore us, that we may live in his presence' (6:1-2, NIV). On the third day, Jesus rose again and, where there was no people, there is a people of God. 'You will be my people and I will be your God.'

And now the message of Jesus goes out from Jerusalem. It went first to Judea and Samaria. Jesus told the first disciples: 'But you will receive power when the Holy Spirit has come upon you, and you will be my witnesses in Jerusalem and in all Judea and Samaria, and to the end of the earth' (Acts 1:8).

Judea was the new name for Judah, and Samaria was the new name of Israel (a name based on its ancient capital). In other words, the Jews were the descendants of the southern kingdom of Judah and the Samaritans were the people that resulted from the mixing of those Israelites who were left in the land with immigrants from other nations. Samaritan religion, too, was a mixture of beliefs, which is why the Jews despised them (John 4:9). But now through the gospel, Jews and Samaritans, Judeans and Israelites, are united in Christ – just as Hosea promised. **The people of Judah and the people of Israel will come together** (1:11, NIV). The apostle John claims that the high priest unwittingly prophesied that Jesus would fulfil Hosea's promise through the cross:

> But one of them, Caiaphas, who was high priest that year, said to them, 'You know nothing at all. Nor do you understand that it is better for you that one man should die for the people, not that the whole nation should perish.' He did not say this of his own accord, but being high priest that year he prophesied that Jesus would die for the nation, and not for the nation only, but also to gather into one the children of God who are scattered abroad. (John 11:49-52)

This is fulfilled in the book of Acts as the gospel goes to Judea and Samaria and people from those regions are united through the cross into one church.

From Judea and Samaria, the message went into Asia and Europe. And then to Africa, and then to the Americas. And people from every nation are becoming God's people through faith in Jesus. Thousands of them. Just as Hosea promised: **Yet the Israelites will be like the sand on the seashore, which cannot be measured or counted** (1:10, NIV).

And somewhere along the line it came to you. It comes to you now – this promise and invitation. Hosea says: **In the place where it was said to them, 'You are not my people', they will be called 'children of the living God'** (1:10, NIV). **Say of your brothers, 'My people', and of your sisters, 'My loved one'** (2:1, NIV).

This is your moment. This is your place in the story. This is where the story can become your story. This is the moment when you can say, 'I am a child of the living God.' This is the moment when you can say, 'I am loved by a heavenly Father.'

Hosea 1:10 (along with 2:23) is quoted by Paul in Romans 9:22-26:

> What if God, desiring to show his wrath and to make known his power, has endured with much patience vessels of wrath prepared for destruction, in order to make known the riches of his glory for vessels of mercy, which he has prepared beforehand for glory – even us whom he has called, not from the Jews only but also from the Gentiles? As indeed he says in Hosea,

> 'Those who were not my people I will call "my people," and her who was not beloved I will call "beloved."'

> 'And in the very place where it was said to them,

> "You are not my people,"

> there they will be called "sons of the living God."'

The fulfilment of God's promise in Hosea 1:10 is the conversion of the Gentiles along with the Jews. Many Israelites were 'vessels of wrath prepared for destruction'. But they did not thwart God's plans or threaten His promises. God is gathering a vast number that cannot be counted to be His people. Hosea makes a promise that the Jews will once again be God's people. Paul applies this to the inclusion of the Gentiles. This is not an arbitrary move or an incidental application. It is important to recognise Paul's logic. Paul is showing that this promise finds its ultimate fulfilment in the inclusion of the Gentiles. This is not a mistake, but goes right to the heart of the meaning of Hosea 1 in the storyline of the Bible. Paul recognises that *the plight of the Gentiles is that of the Jews*. In other words, Israel in exile is a picture of humanity in exile. But he also recognises that *the plight of the Jews is now that of the Gentiles*. In other words, Israel has stepped outside the covenant blessing and received the covenant curses. She who was 'my people' has become **not my people**. Israel has become Gentile. And there is no way back through covenant keeping, through works of the law or through ethnic identity. Israel could not again become God's people by being Israel. They are in exactly the same boat as Gentiles. The only route back is the mercy of God and faithfulness of His true Son. But if Israelites can be saved through faith rather than their Jewish identity, then there is no reason why Gentiles cannot also be saved in the same way. If Jews will be saved not through their ethnic identity but despite it, then Gentiles can also be saved despite their ethnic identity. What counts is the electing love of God and faith in Christ. David Starling concludes: 'Gentiles can become "my people" because Israel has first become "not my people".'[5] The promise of 1:10 that **not my people** can be God's people must apply to both Jews and Gentiles alike.

And so still the story is not over. For a day is coming when God will place His people in a world made new. Hosea says: **The people ... will come up out of the land, for great will be the day of Jezreel** (1:11, NIV). Jehu was supposed to have purged Israel at Jezreel. The blood of judgment fell on the dynasty of Ahab and Israel was free. But, under Jehu, Israel had returned to her sin. So another day of Jezreel, another day of bloodshed, is promised in verse 5. Could this be a reference to the cross? Judgment again falls at the cross. Again there is bloodshed. Again there is purging. But this time it is complete and finished and enduring. This time the day of bloodshed is great. From this blood flows healing and restoration for people from all nations. The earth itself is renewed. Verse 11 says: **And they shall go up from the land**. This *going up* from the land is not a reference to exile, but to resurrection. There will be a rising up, a resurrection. It is echoed by Ezekiel in his famous vision of dry bones (Ezek. 37). The resurrection of Jesus is the promise and beginning of a resurrection for all God's people and the promise and beginning of the renewal of all things.

Who are you in the story?

So *who* are you in the story? Perhaps you are **Jezreel**. Perhaps you are indifferent to God, happy to ignore Him, happy to have other priorities in life, happy to love other things. Jezreel is a warning that your future is bloodshed.

Or perhaps you feel like **Lo-Ruhamah**, Unloved. Unloved by people. Unloved by God. Maybe you feel like **Lo-Ammi**,

5.   David I. Starling, *Not My People: Gentiles as Exiles in Pauline Hermeneutics*, Berlin, De Gruyter, 2011, 164.

Not My People. You believe God is Creator, maybe even Saviour. But He does not feel like *your* God and you do not feel like His child. If He is a Father then he is distant Father.

God says to you today: You **will be called "children of the living God"** (1:10, NIV). God tells me to say to you, **'say of your brothers,' He says, '"My people", and of your sisters, "My loved one"'** (2:1, NIV). So I say to you, 'You are God's People. You are God's Loved Ones.'

Some readers will have had great fathers, fathers who loved you, protected you, disciplined you well, played with you. Think of all that is good about your father. This is what God is like to you – only better, more loving, more protecting, more wise in His discipline. Some of you had bad fathers, fathers who left you or who were absent or fathers who were cruel, maybe even abusive. God is the Father you always wished you had.

Do not take matters into your own hands. That is what Israel did in verse 7 when they trusted in their bows and horsemen. Do not look for affirmation elsewhere. There is a high correlation between absentee fathers and teenage pregnancy. Missing the affirmation of their fathers, girls seek to find male approval through sex. We can do a spiritual version of this. If we do not rest in the approval of our heavenly Father, we look to establish our own affirmation and approval. People may do a religious version of this and look for approval through good works or religious duties. But secular people also do this through career success, good looks, material possessions, and so on.

But God is not an absentee father. So we do not need to act like orphans. Galatians 4:4-7 says: 'But when the time had fully come, God sent his Son, born of a woman, born under law, to redeem those under law, that we might receive the full rights of sons. Because you are sons, God sent the Spirit of his Son into our hearts, the Spirit who calls out, "Abba, Father". So you are no longer a slave, but a son; and since you are a son, God has made you also an heir.' God the Father not only sends His Son that you might be adopted into his family, He also sends His Spirit so that you might *know* that you are adopted. It is not sufficient for God the Father to make you His child. He wants you to *feel* you are a child of the living God. So cry out to the Spirit to make you alive to His cry in you of 'Abba, Father', to make you feel like a child of God, to have the confidence of a child, to feel the protection of your heavenly Father, to know that you are loved by your Father, to know that you are accepted by your Father, to strut your stuff in the world as an heir of God.

The famous parable of the prodigal son tells the story of a lost son who is reunited with his father. It is a picture of the welcome our heavenly Father extends to sinners. It, too, involves a resurrection. In Hosea 1:11, God's people **shall go up from the land**, rising as it were out of the ashes of God's judgment. In the same way, in the parable of the prodigal the father says: 'For this my son was dead, and is alive again; he was lost, and is found' (Luke 15:24).

STUDY QUESTIONS

1. What are some of the ways in which people today are unfaithful to God?

2. What are some of the ways in which the church today is unfaithful to God?

3. How do you think Hosea's neighbours might have responded to the announcement of the names of his children?

4. What names might bring the challenge of the gospel to your culture?

5. Hosea 1:10 is a promise first made by Hosea to the Jews. But in Romans 9:22-26 Paul applies it to the inclusion of the Gentiles in the people of God. Explain Paul's logic.

6. Give examples from your experience of the gospel uniting disparate people under one head.

Questions for Personal Reflection

1. Who are you in the story? What is Hosea's message to you?

2. In 2:1 God tells Hosea what to say to his fellow Israelites. Whom do you know who needs to hear these words: 'You are my people' and 'You have received mercy'?

2

God Displays His Jealousy
(Hosea 2:2-13)

Do you ever think, 'God's grace means it doesn't matter if I sin because God will forgive me anyway'? I suspect we all think some version of this from time to time. In fact, there is a sense in which if you have never thought like this then you may never have really understood the radical nature of gospel grace. We are forgiven, justified, acquitted by faith alone – not because of what we do, but despite what we do. Grace covers past, present and future sins. Even as I sin I can be confident that I am justified.

So does sin matter? The answer of Hosea 2 is an emphatic Yes. For sin is not simply breaking God's law. It is breaking God's heart.

Israel pursues her lovers (2:2-5)

In chapter 1, Hosea was told to marry 'an adulterous wife' (1:2, NIV). Now in chapter 2 it is God Himself who is married to an adulterous wife. Hosea 2:2 says: **Plead with your mother, plead – for she is not my wife, and I am not her husband – that she put away her whoring from her face, and her adultery from between her breasts**. This takes us to the heart of Hosea's message. God is passionate about His people. And one feature of this passion is that He is wounded by His people's unfaithfulness.

There is a strong and important forensic or legal aspect to salvation. Sin is a violation of God's law. There will be a final judgment. There will be, as it were, a court case. The evidence against us will be examined and weighed. The guilty verdict is already clear. But God Himself has intervened. The sentence God's people deserve has already been carried out on Jesus at the cross. He has borne the penalty of our sin. The verdict that our lives deserve is taken by Jesus. And the verdict that His life deserved is given to us. He bears the judgment against our disobedience while we enjoy the rewards of His obedience. Through Christ, the justice of God is satisfied even as He acquits His guilty people. This is the explanation of salvation that we read in Romans 3. This is, as it were, the legal underpinning of our salvation. Through the cross, God demonstrates His justice 'so that he might be just and the justifier of the one who has faith in Jesus' (Rom. 3:26).

But our salvation is not simply a legal transaction. Salvation is not just an act of justice. It is also an act of love. God is betrayed by our sin. But, whereas you or I might respond to betrayal with resentment or spite or anger, God responds with mercy. He is not an impartial Judge in the sky, coldly calculating legal intricacies. He is a jilted lover. He feels our betrayal. He is passionate about His people.

Your in verse 2 refers to individuals within Israel, **she** refers to Israel as a collective identity and **my** refers to God. God is not addressing the nation as a whole directly. Instead, he addresses individuals within the nation. In one sense, it is an invitation for individual Israelites to distance themselves from the national spiritual direction. It creates a space for individuals to turn in repentance towards God.

But the rhetorical force is more like this. Imagine a scene in which the relationship between a husband and wife has broken down to such an extent that the wife will no longer talk to her husband. So instead he must ask his children to pass on messages. In a similar way, God addresses individuals within Israel, the children of the nation. Perhaps you can recall comedy programmes where a husband says in hearing of his wife, 'Tell your mother I'm going out.' And before the child can pass on the message, the mother says, 'You can tell your father not to expect any dinner when he comes home.' But there is nothing comic about this scene.

God is *pleading* with Israel in verse 2:

'Plead with your mother, plead ...
that she put away her whoring from her face,
and her adultery from between her breasts ...'

And God is *warning* Israel in verses 3-4:

... lest I strip her naked
and make her as in the day she was born,
and make her like a wilderness,
and make her like a parched land,
and kill her with thirst.
Upon her children also I will have no mercy,
because they are children of whoredom.

The statement **for she is not my wife and I am not her husband** could be a question: **Plead with your mother, plead – for is she not my wife and am I not her husband?** This softens the implication in the ESV and NIV that the marriage has irrevocably broken down which the rest of the chapter shows is not the case. But the translation **she is not my wife and I am not her husband** is perhaps better understood rhetorically along the lines of 'it's as if she's not my wife' or 'she's not acting like my wife'.

The call in verse 2 to **put away her whoring from her face, and her adultery from between her breasts** is probably a reference to the jewellery or adornments that would indicate a woman's sexual availability. Verse 13 says: 'And I will punish her for the feast days of the Baals when she burned offerings to them and adorned herself with her ring and jewellery, and went after her lovers and forgot me, declares the LORD.' Her ring and her jewellery were what she wore to seduce her lovers. It is a metaphor for Israel's willingness to follow other gods.

1. Israel forgets her past blessings (2:3-4)
Underlying Israel's adultery are two sad realities: she is forgetting her past blessings (3-4) and misunderstanding her present blessings (5).

Verse 3 reminds us of Israel's origins and God's blessing from the beginning of her history: **lest I strip her naked and make her as in the day she was born, and make her like a wilderness, and make her like a parched land, and kill her with thirst.** The immediate reference is to a baby. God will strip her naked so she is like a newly born baby. Just as a baby enters the world with nothing, so God will remove Israel's blessings so that she has nothing left. But Israel was birthed as a nation in the wilderness when Moses brought them to Mount Sinai to make a covenant with God. God rescued the descendants of Jacob from slavery in Egypt and led them into the desert. In Hosea 11, God speaks very tenderly of nurturing Israel as a young child: 'When Israel was a child, I loved him, and out of Egypt I called my son … it was I who taught Ephraim to walk; I took them up by their arms' (11:1, 3). In the wilderness at Mount Sinai, Israel was formed as an independent nation. This was the moment when she became more than an extended family and when she was no longer a slave people.

But more than that, Israel was formed as a nation in a covenant relationship with God. She became not only a nation, but a *holy* nation (Exod. 19:4-6). In other words, she was a nation distinct from any other nation because she was God's covenant people. She was set apart for God. It was in a sense a marriage. The covenant at Mount Sinai was the marriage covenant that bound God to His people and his people to Him. But now that marriage covenant is broken. Israel is an adulterous wife (2:2) and her children are **the children of adultery** (2:4, NIV)

Israel has forgotten what God has done for her in the past. She has forgotten her identity. She is not living as God's wife. So God is going to rewind the story. Taken together, the two halves of verse 3 suggest God is going to take Israel back to where He found her. Not only will she go back to the wilderness, but she herself will be a wilderness. The reference to thirst recalls Exodus 17:1-7 and Numbers 20:2-13 when Israel experienced thirst in the wilderness. At Mount Sinai, Israel's identity changed. She became a holy nation, set apart for God. She became God's wife. But she has forgotten her identity.

Remembering our new identity remains as important as ever for God's people. Think for a moment how you would summarise Ephesians 5:1 in your own words: *'Be imitators of God, as beloved children.'* I wonder whether your summary focused on the call to imitate God or whether it focused on the description of Christians as 'beloved children'? It is all too easy for us to hear only the commands of Scripture and miss the descriptions out of which they arise. The prescription to behave like God only makes sense as the outworking of the description that we have a new identity as God's children. The imperatives (the commands) of the Bible always arise out of the indicatives (the descriptions). We are already God's dearly loved children, so we can live as God's dearly loved children by imitating our Father.

In the world around us our identity (who we are) arises out of our activity (what we do). In other words, who I am is based on what I do. I am a successful person if I succeed. I am an attractive person if I am cool. I am a good mother if I have lovely children. I am a professional if I gain the necessary qualifications. The mercy of God turns the world's way upside down. In the world our identity must be achieved. In the gospel it is generously given to us in Christ. As a result, in the gospel our activity (what we do) arises out of our identity (who we are). God makes me a good person (a person declared righteous in His sight), then I do good works.

You cannot make a tree into an apple tree by gluing apples on to it. But if a tree is an apple tree then it will produce apples. In the same way, my good works do not make me who I am. Instead they are the natural expression of who I am as a result of God's work. You cannot make yourself a good person by gluing good works on to your life. But if you are united to Christ, then you will produce good works.

God's complaint against Israel was not that they had not done enough to become His wife. He was not expecting them to win His heart by their beauty or love. He was not expecting activity to lead to identity (being His wife). No, He had graciously rescued them, loved them and made them His wife. He had graciously made a covenant with them that set them apart as His people. But He did expect identity to lead to activity. He expected their identity as His bride to lead to actions of love.

It is the same for Christians. God does not expect us to win His heart or earn His approval. We already have His approval in Christ. We are already the bride of Christ for whom He gave His life. Our problems arise when we forget this identity. Living holy lives is not about trying hard to become something we are not. It is about remembering who we already are in Christ and living in the light of that reality. And we encourage one another to live holy lives by reminding one another who we already are in Christ.

Not only do we have a new identity, but that new identity was given to us through the cross. So living holy lives is also about remembering God's love to us in Christ. Our new identity was won by Christ through the shedding of His own blood. I know in my own experience that grace encourages me to sin *only when I think of grace as an abstract idea*. What I mean is this. God's grace is His undeserved love and forgiveness. We are loved even though we sin and even when we sin. We are forgiven despite our past, present and future sins. All this is gloriously true. But I find myself reasoning in this way when I face temptation: 'This sin will not matter because grace means I will be forgiven' or 'This sin will have no consequences in my life because of grace.' And this reasoning has traction in my heart. I find it persuasive. But *only* if I think of grace in the abstract as a 'thing'.

Sometimes the Bible does personify grace. Titus 2:11, for example, says 'For the grace of God has appeared, bringing salvation for all people.' But this is a rhetorical device. Grace is not a principle or law. Still less is it a thing or substance. Grace is the attitude and action *of a person*. When Titus 2 says grace appeared, it is a way of saying *Jesus* appeared. So the statement 'grace means I will be forgiven' is actually shorthand for 'God in His grace will forgive me through the death of Christ'. And it is very hard to attach the clause 'so this sin will not matter' to that statement! The consequences of my sin are made explicit. I may not experience the consequences of my sin, but only because my Saviour experienced them on the cross. Now I see my sin is not an act against an impersonal law with no consequences. Now I see my sin as an act against a person and not just any person, but 'the Son of God, who loved me and gave himself for me' (Gal. 2:20).

This brings us back to the heart of Hosea's messages in chapter two: Sin is not simply breaking God's law. It is breaking God's heart.

2. Israel mistakes her present blessings (2:5, 8)

In verses 3-4, Israel is adulterous because she has forgotten her past blessings. In verse 5, she is adulterous because she has misunderstood her present blessings:

> For their mother has played the whore;
>> she who conceived them has acted shamefully.
> For she said, "I will go after my lovers,
>> who give me my bread and my water,
>> my wool and my flax, my oil and my drink." (2:5)

Imagine a wife married to a poor, humble worker. Times are hard and their life together is a struggle. Then she catches the eye of a rich businessman. He showers her with gifts, all the luxuries her husband cannot afford to give her. So she responds to his advances. He offers her so much more than her husband can offer. She chooses a life of security and luxury with her lover over a life of fear and poverty with her husband. Her actions, at least, have a certain mercenary logic to them.

And this is the logic that Israel has been applying. She has gone after her **lovers** – that is, other gods. And the reason she gives for this infidelity is that they give her bread, water, wool, flax, oil and drink. In verse 12, Israel says of her vines and fig trees, **These are my wages, which my lovers have given me**. She attributed her success to her devotion to Baal.

This is a reference to the fertility cult of Baal. Baal was the god of the Canaanites, the original inhabitants of the land whom Israel should have driven out, but many of whom remained (Judg. 1–2). At the heart of the Baal pantheon was Hadad, the god of rain and storm. He was manifest through local baals in shrines and high places. The baals 'impregnated' the land, the mother goddess, with rain to make it fertile. Baal worship included shrine prostitution in which worshippers enacted the marriage of Baal with the earth. Baal could also be portrayed as a warrior who each year fought with death to ensure another harvest.

So Baal was seen as the source of all fertility and worshipping him would ensure the good harvests upon which prosperity in an agricultural society depended. This is why Israel attributes bread and water to him. Baal worship was a perennial threat for Israel. Each cycle of the agricultural year represented a new temptation to look to Baal for provision. So Israel's logic was this: 'Baal is a fertility god. We need fertility. We need Baal. We will "go after" Baal.'

But, quite apart from the corrosive infidelity at its heart, the premise of this logic is utterly flawed. For it is not Baal who provides for Israel, but the LORD. The scenario is more akin to a devoted husband who wraps up a diamond necklace and places it under the Christmas tree. But when his wife opens it on Christmas Day she concludes it is a gift from her lover. In verse 8, Yahweh says:

> And she did not know
> that it was I who gave her
> the grain, the wine, and the oil,
> and who lavished on her silver and gold,
> which they used for Baal. (2:8)

It was I who gave ... and who lavished on her ... The construction is emphatic. It has the sense of 'It was I and I alone.' It was not Baal. It was not even some blessing from Baal and some from the LORD. It is the LORD and the LORD alone who has blessed Israel. And nor has the LORD simply provided for Israel. He has **lavished** blessings on her. Hosea takes the language of the Baal cult and subverts it. He takes the ideas of other religions and co-opts them to speak of God and His goodness.

To what in our day do we attribute our blessings?

- 'Wall Street or the City of London are the source of our prosperity.'

- 'We're successful as a nation because we have a liberal democracy.'

- 'The free market is the engine of a successful economy.'

- 'Our only hope is government intervention.'

- 'I've got where I am today through hard work and initiative.'

- 'Get yourself a good education and that will set you up for life.'

Of course, there is truth in all these statements – just as it was true to say that Israel depended on the land for her prosperity. But they are only partial truths. They represent the perspective of a culture that believes in a closed universe, a world in which all you see is all you get. And that perspective can affect our thinking in the church. We too can attribute blessing to, or look for hope in, the market or the government or our own hard work without recognising that these are simply some of the means that God uses to bless us. We can sing God's praise on a Sunday and then be 'functional atheists' throughout the week. In other words, if God has no impact on our attitude to work, politics or education then, whatever we might think in theory, we are functioning as if He does not exist.

Verse 13 says Israel **'went after her lovers, but me she forgot,'** declares the LORD (NIV). 'Me she forgot.' No doubt the people of Israel still remembered God's name. They could still tell the stories of Abraham, Moses and David. But they were suffering from 'practical amnesia'. They were forgetting God in day-to-day life. They were living as if He did not exist or as if Baal was more important.

The painful twist in the story is that Israel not only attributes her blessings to Baal when in fact they come from God, but then she takes the blessings that have come from God and uses them to honour Baal. God **lavished on her silver and gold, which they used for Baal** (2:8). Instead of returning thanks to God, they made offerings to Baal.

What should Israel have done when she enjoyed good harvests? How should we react when we are successful? Psalm 65 offers a model. Inspired by the Holy Spirit, David shows how we should interpret our blessings and how we should respond? You might want to pray through this Psalm, taking each verse and using it as a basis for your own praise and prayer.

Praise is due to you, O God, in Zion,
   and to you shall vows be performed.
²O you who hears prayer,
   to you shall all flesh come.
³When iniquities prevail against me,
   you atone for our transgressions.
⁴Blessed is the one you choose and bring near,
   to dwell in your courts!
We shall be satisfied with the goodness of your house,
   the holiness of your temple!
⁵By awesome deeds you answer us with righteousness,
   O God of our salvation,
the hope of all the ends of the earth
   and of the farthest seas;
⁶the one who by his strength established the mountains,
   being girded with might;
⁷who stills the roaring of the seas,
   the roaring of their waves,
   the tumult of the peoples,
⁸so that those who dwell at the ends of the earth
   are in awe at your signs.
You make the going out of the morning
   and the evening to shout for joy.
⁹You visit the earth and water it;
   you greatly enrich it;
the river of God is full of water;
   you provide their grain,
   for so you have prepared it.
¹⁰You water its furrows abundantly,
   settling its ridges,
softening it with showers,
   and blessing its growth.
¹¹You crown the year with your bounty;
   your wagon tracks overflow with abundance.
¹²The pastures of the wilderness overflow,
   the hills gird themselves with joy,
¹³the meadows clothe themselves with flocks,
   the valleys deck themselves with grain,
   they shout and sing together for joy.

God pursues His bride by withdrawing His blessings (2:6-13)
Jane says: 'I'm devastated. I've given everything to my career and now they've made me redundant.' Pete says: 'I'll tell you

why I use porn. I've prayed and prayed for a wife and God's not given one to me. That's why I use porn.'

You may have heard sentiments like these. You may have uttered them yourself – or at least thought them in your darker moments. These people do not feel blessed by God. In fact, they feel let down by God. They feel as if God has not kept His side of the bargain. They have served Him and He has not rewarded their service.

But could it be their struggles are in fact a sign of God's love towards them? Could it be that sometimes problems are God's blessing in disguise?

Look at how verses 6 and 9-13 begin: **I will block ... I will take away ... I will expose ... I will stop ... I will ruin ... I will punish ...** (NIV). God pursues His bride by withdrawing His blessings. Strange as it may seem, God sometimes blesses us by removing His blessing. He prevents us finding satisfaction in other lovers. He wants to bring us to our senses.

This is what Moses had warned the people God would do. In Deuteronomy 8, as the people are about to take possession of the Promised Land, Moses warns them not to be led astray by prosperity. They must not be so preoccupied with their wealth that they forget God, nor must they claim the credit for what God has given them. Poverty is a threat to our physical well-being. But wealth can be a threat to our spiritual well-being if we do not give thanks to God. So later in Deuteronomy, Moses says: 'Because you did not serve the LORD your God joyfully and gladly in the time of prosperity, therefore in hunger and thirst, in nakedness and dire poverty, you will serve the enemies the LORD sends against you. He will put an iron yoke on your neck until he has destroyed you' (28:47-48).

Food, clothing and intimacy were the three things a wife could expect under the law of Moses: 'If he takes another wife to himself, he shall not diminish her food, her clothing, or her marital rights.' (Exod. 21:10) But now God will take them away from Israel.

The **thornbushes** in verse 6 were often trained over walls to prevent animals escaping or thieves breaking in. **Therefore I will block her path with thornbushes; I will wall her in so that she cannot find her way**. They were, in effect, the barbed-wire fencing of our day. So God is saying He will keep Israel from her lovers with a wall topped with barbed wire.

In verses 2-3, God said: **Plead with your mother ... lest I strip her naked.** In verse 9, he says: **I will take away my wool and my flax which were to cover her nakedness.** In verse 10, God is even more direct: **Now I will uncover her lewdness in the sight of her lovers.** But this is more than emptying her wardrobe or cutting up her store card. This is an act of shaming. God is taking away her reputation. She is exposed. The reality of her sin is laid bare. We can hide our sin behind a cloak of respectability. But God sees our hearts. Romans 2:16 says that on the last day 'God judges the secrets of men by Christ Jesus'. 2 Peter 3:10 says that in the last day 'the heavens will pass away with a roar, and the heavenly bodies will be burned up and dissolved, and the earth and the works that are done on it will be exposed.' One day we will all be stripped naked and our hearts will be exposed before God's judgment. It is therefore a great blessing to be stripped bare *before* that day so we can recognise our sin and have the opportunity to repent. That can happen through the circumstances of our lives, as it would for Israel. But it can also happen through the Spirit as we read God's Word. Hebrews 4:12-13 says: 'For the word of God is living and active, sharper than any two-edged sword, piercing to the division of soul and of spirit, of joints and of marrow, and discerning the thoughts and intentions of the heart. And no creature is hidden from his sight, but all are naked and exposed to the eyes of him to whom we must give account.'

As we have seen, verse 8 says Israel interpreted the provision of food as a sign that the Baal fertility cult was effective. But, in fact, it was an expression of God's generosity. Now in verse 9 God says He will unpick all the blessings of verse 8. The warning that God will **take away my grain when it ripens** (NIV) probably refers to invading armies rather than bad harvest (Deut. 28:18). Armies typically went to war at harvest time so that they would have provisions while on their military campaign and so that they could inflict maximum economic damage. The LORD does not say there will be no harvest. The corn will ripen and the wine will be ready. But that harvest will be taken away just when it is bountiful by the invading Assyrian armies.

Why does God bless His people by withdrawing blessing? Because He wants us to recognise not only that blessings come from Him, but that *He Himself* is the true blessing.

The reality is that Israel was not interested in God. She was interested in food, wealth, possessions. If she thought Baal was the best bet for getting more stuff, then she would opt for Baal. And if she thought the LORD was the best bet for getting more stuff, then she would opt for the LORD. That seems to be what is happening in verse 7:

> She shall pursue her lovers
>   but not overtake them,
> and she shall seek them
>   but shall not find them.
> Then she shall say,
>   'I will go and return to my first husband,
>   for it was better for me then than now.'

At first sight, this might look like Israel is ready to return to God. It looks like she is doing just what God pleaded with her to do in verse 2: to put away her adultery and return to Him. But the last line is the giveaway: **for it was better for me then than now.** She does not want God. She just wants His blessings. She wants His stuff. She is like a woman who marries a man for his wealth. When another man comes along promising more wealth, she becomes his lover. When that wealth does not materialise, she returns to her husband. Whom does she love? The reality is she never loved her husband or her lover. She only ever loved herself. That is Israel. God wants her to look beyond His blessings to God Himself. But she looks beyond God to His blessings.

In Amos 4, God speaks of a gift He gave to His people: 'empty stomachs' (Amos 4:6). He 'withheld rain' so that 'people staggered from town to town for water' (Amos 4:7-8). He struck their crops with mildew (Amos 4:9). These might seem strange gifts! But God gives them so that His people might repent. They are terrible things, but idolatry and its consequences are worse. God always seeks the best for His people and that best is Himself. Famine and thirst are acts of divine love when their aim is to bring us back to God.

This is the message Jane and Pete need to hear. Jane has made an idol of her career and Peter has made an idol of marriage. Both work and marriage are good things. But when something matters more to us than God – even a good thing – then it has become an idol. One sign of whether these good desires have become idolatrous desires is what happens when they are taken away. Jane is left devastated. Pete turns to porn. Neither of them are satisfied in God. God is either marginal to their lives or they see Him as the means to get the things they really want.

But God will not bless our idolatry. He may strip us of our idols so that we pursue Him. God is the ultimate blessing. He is very generous. But He wants us to pursue Him for Himself and not just pursue Him for His blessing. It may be that God is blessing Jane and Pete by withdrawing His blessings so that they will discover the greater blessing of being satisfied in God.

Study Questions

1. Why does it matter when Christians sin? How does Hosea 2 help us answer this question?

2. How does God respond to our sin?

3. How do people today try to achieve a sense of identity? What fruit does this produce in their lives?

4. To what do people in your context attribute their present blessings?

5. How should we respond when we are successful?

6. Give examples from your experience of God blessing people by withdrawing His blessing.

Questions for Personal Reflection

1. Do your problems ever eclipse your sense of God's blessing to you?

2. Do you ever think of grace as a 'thing' rather than God's personal, undeserved and costly love to you?

3. Do you ever think, 'Grace means it doesn't matter if I sin because I'll be forgiven'?

4. How does Hosea 2 help you think about these issues aright?

3

God Reclaims His Bride
(Hosea 2:14–3:5)

In Luke 15, Jesus famously tells a parable about a prodigal son who demands his share of his father's inheritance even while his father is still alive. Then the son leaves home and wastes his wealth. As a result, he ends up destitute, looking after pigs and wishing he could eat their food. Hosea 2 tells the story of the prodigal wife. Israel is God's bride. But she has taken the blessings God has given her and lavished them on other lovers. She has left home, as it were, and gone off after other gods. But God will no longer indulge her profligacy. She will be left naked and destitute when the Assyrian army invades. God's marriage to His people is on the rocks because of their unfaithfulness.

Tim Keller has suggested that the story of the prodigal son is misnamed. The word 'prodigal' means recklessly wasteful. The son is prodigal because he wastes the inheritance he has received. But the real focus of the narrative is the father, and the father is reckless and wasteful in the love he lavishes on his returning son. The same is true of the story of the prodigal wife in Hosea 2. Perhaps it is really the story of the prodigal husband. For the second half of the chapter describes how God will win back His wayward bride and renew His blessing on her. In chapter 3, Hosea then enacts this message as he himself buys back his wife Gomer from the slave market.

A renewed love (2:14-15)

This section begins with the word **Therefore**. It reveals a strange logic. The word 'therefore' introduces an action that is the logical consequence of whatever has just been described. 'It's raining. Therefore, I'm going to put my coat on.' Putting your coat on is the logical consequence of rain. In verse 13, God says, 'I will punish her for the feast days when she ... went after her lovers and forgot me.' Then He says 'therefore'. What would you expect to come next? Perhaps something like 'Therefore she will be desolate and destroyed'. That is what you might expect having read the word 'therefore' in verses 6 and 9 where in each case it connected sin with judgment. So the word 'therefore' at the beginning of verse 14 leads us to expect more judgment.

But instead we get *the logic of divine grace* in which God's judgment becomes the occasion for God's mercy. This literary device reflects reality: God's grace is surprising. God's grace is surprising by very definition. God's grace is His undeserved favour. So whenever it arrives, it comes as a surprise. It is surprising because God shows grace when and where He should show judgment. And it is surprising because the people upon whom He shows grace are undeserving. So this is what God actually says:

> 14'Therefore, behold, I will allure her,
>   and bring her into the wilderness,
>   and speak tenderly to her.
> 15And there I will give her her vineyards
>   and make the Valley of Achor a door of hope.
> And there she shall answer as in the days of her youth,
>   as at the time when she came out of the land of Egypt.'

Imagine a husband whose marriage is in trouble. The relationship between him and his wife is strained to breaking. In one final attempt to get things back on track, he takes his wife back to the place where they first fell in love. Perhaps here she will remember why she first loved him and the old feelings can be rekindled.

This is what God is doing in these verses. God and His people had entered into a covenant relationship (they had, in effect, married) when God made a covenant with them through

Moses at Mount Sinai after He had rescued them from Egypt. Now God wants to take them back to those beginnings. He is going to win her love all over again.

While Hosea is ministering in the northern kingdom of Israel, God tells Jeremiah to proclaim a similar message in the southern kingdom of Judah: 'Go and proclaim in the hearing of Jerusalem, Thus says the LORD, "I remember the devotion of your youth, your love as a bride, how you followed me in the wilderness, in a land not sown. Israel was holy to the LORD, the firstfruits of his harvest"' (Jer. 2:2-3).

The desert was not only the place where God's covenant relationship with Israel had begun. It was also the place where His provision was clear and unambiguous. The wilderness was a place of training or testing. It was the place where God got Egypt out of His people's blood, as it were. Now God is going to do that again. There were no fertility gods in the desert. That is the nature of a desert. By definition it is unfertile. Yet there in the desert God provided for His people in remarkable ways. Exodus 16 describes how God provided bread from heaven. Exodus 17 describes how God provided water from rock. And when the people complain about even this, Numbers 11 describes how He provided quails on the wind. Any god, we might say, can provide for you in fertile countryside. But only the LORD can provide for you in a desert!

> This means nothing less than that God is going to take them back to the place where he originally began with them, back, as it were, at the beginning of the whole road. There, in the wilderness, no gods of fertility can come between Jahweh and his people; there Israel will be thrown back completely upon Jahweh; Jahweh will have her all to himself, in order that from the desert he can once more grace her the land.[1]

This is the first hint in Hosea that God will accomplish a second exodus. The exodus from Egypt was the great, defining act of redemption in Israel's history. Now it becomes the pattern for a greater future act of salvation. Just as God rescued His people from slavery to Pharaoh and made her His covenant

---

1.   von Rad, *Old Testament Theology Volume II*, 146.

people, so God will again rescue his people from slavery to sin and make a new covenant with her.

The Valley of Achor had a particular resonance for the people of Israel. Achor was the name they gave to the place where Achan was executed. When Israel first entered the land of Canaan, God promised to fight for them and give them the land. As a sign of this, they were not to take any of the booty of war. Normally booty went to the victor. But Israel was not the true victor; God was. But an Israelite named Achan could not resist taking some of the spoils of the victory over Jericho. He took a cloak plus some silver and gold, and hid them in his tent. So God judged His people by allowing them to be defeated by the relatively weak city of Ai. As a result, Achan's sin was exposed and he was executed.

> Joshua said, 'Why did you bring trouble on us? The LORD brings trouble on you today.' And all Israel stoned him with stones. They burned them with fire and stoned them with stones. Over Achan they heaped up a large pile of rocks, which remains to this day. Then the LORD turned from his fierce anger. Therefore that place has been called the Valley of Achor ever since (Josh. 7:25-26).

Names in the Bible are often significant, particularly when the act of naming is part of the story, as it is here. Achor means 'trouble' – literally and symbolically. It represents sin (Achan's sin), defeat (Israel's defeat) and judgment (God's judgment against Achan). All of that is about to be replayed in Israel's history. Like Achan, Israel has coveted material possessions and disobeyed God. Like Israel of old, she is about to be defeated (this time by the Assyrians). Like Achan, she is about to be judged by God.

Achor means trouble. But now God is going to make even Achor a door of hope. Israel had passed through the Valley of Achor as they entered the Promised Land. Now again Achor will be the doorway to a new life. Sin, defeat and judgment will not be the end of the story. They will be a route to a new beginning.

How is this fulfilled? It is worth thinking about whom Hosea is addressing through these words. He addresses Israel, the northern kingdom, as a nation. But for them there was no hope. They would be defeated by the Assyrians and all but lost to history. But we have already seen in verse 2 that Hosea also addresses individuals within the nation (the children of God's bride). Israel as a whole may not repent, but individual Israelites might respond to Hosea's message.

But the northern kingdom of Israel was not the only entity who were God's people. Away in the south was the estranged kingdom of Judah. We do not know who recorded Hosea's words. But, with the northern kingdom in disarray, it is likely the intended first *readers* of Hosea were people in the kingdom of Judah. Hosea addresses himself to the northern kingdom of Israel. But the compiler of his words wants Judah to learn from his message to Israel. They, too, are facing God's judgment and need to repent.

But they too as a whole would not repent. They, too, would be defeated and exiled, this time by the Babylonians. However, this would not be the end of the story. God would be faithful to His promises. A remnant would return. As we saw when we looked at Hosea 1, God's people would limp on until we reach the time of Christ. Christ is the true faithful people of God. He is our representative. But what happens to Him, the true people of God? 'Achor'. 'Trouble'. He is made sin for us, and He experiences defeat and judgment. On the cross, the people of God are utterly defeated and destroyed. But the Valley of Achor becomes **a door of hope**. On the third day, Jesus rises again. His death is our death, the death we deserve. His resurrection is our life, the reward He deserves.

The lovers in this chapter are those I love rather than those who love me. There is no affection from the lovers, no longing, no concern, no kindness. Israel's so-called lovers only exploit and abuse her. But God is very different. **Speak tenderly** in verse 14 is literally 'speak to her heart'. Israel's other lovers are interested in what they can get from the relationship. God is interested in what He can give to it. Tim Keller says, 'Jesus is the only Lord who, if you receive him, will fulfil you completely, and, if you fail him, will forgive you eternally.'[2]

---

2.   Timothy Keller, *The Reason for God: Belief in an Age of Skepticism*, Dutton, 2008, 173.

A renewed marriage (2:16-20)

> [16]And in that day, declares the LORD, you will call me 'My Husband,' and no longer will you call me 'My Baal'. [17] For I will remove the names of the Baals from her mouth, and they shall be remembered by name no more. [18]And I will make for them a covenant on that day with the beasts of the field, the birds of the heavens, and the creeping things of the ground. And I will abolish the bow, the sword, and war from the land, and I will make you lie down in safety. [19]And I will betroth you to me for ever. I will betroth you to me in righteousness and in justice, in steadfast love and in mercy. [20]I will betroth you to me in faithfulness. And you shall know the LORD.

Verse 16 is a play on words. The words **My Baal** literally mean 'My Master' or 'My Lord' or 'My Owner'. So, while the ESV translates the end of the verse as **no longer will you call me 'My Baal'**, the NIV translates it as **you will no longer call me 'my master'**. 'Baal' was a generic term for God and could be used of the LORD (Esh-Baal in 1 Chronicles 8:33 means 'man of God'; Merib-Baal in 1 Chronicles 8:34 means 'the Lord defend me'; and Beeliada in 1 Chronicles 14:7 means 'the Lord knows'). But Baal was the term particularly used for Canaanite gods.

So the verse has a double meaning. It means Israel will no longer say that Baal is their god. Verse 17 goes on: **For I will remove the names of the Baals from her mouth, and they shall be remembered by name no more.** When they talk about God, it will no longer be Baal they have in mind, but the LORD. Verse 20 says: **I will betroth you to me in faithfulness. And you shall know the LORD.** The word 'LORD' here is 'Yahweh', the name God revealed to Moses at the burning bush in Exodus 3. It is God's unique *name*. Just as I am a man called 'Tim', so He is God called 'Yahweh' or 'the LORD'.

But verse 16 is also an expression of intimacy. The word that will replace 'Baal' is not simply another word for 'Lord'. They will no longer call God 'my master', but **my husband**. So this has a double meaning. The people will no longer say that God is 'Baal' in the sense of the god of the Canaanites. But they will not even call the true God 'Baal' or 'Master' because they will relate to Him as a wife to a husband. Their relationship will be much more intimate and affectionate.

Imagine a woman who is going to marry her boss. For years in the office, she has called him 'Sir'. That is what she is used to saying. But as they look forward to their wedding day, he says to her, 'On that day you will call me "my husband", and no longer will you call me "my boss". No longer will you say, "Would like a cup of tea, sir?" Instead you will say, "Would you like a cup of tea, *dear*?"' This is God's' invitation to Israel. It is an invitation to think of God differently: not simply as a distant Lord, but as a loving husband.

As God renews His relationship with His people (so they again call Him 'my husband'), their relationship with other lovers will end. Verses 16 and 19-20 are a renewal of marriage vows.

I will betroth you is repeated three times in verses 19-20. In Hebrew grammar, a repetition is a sign of intensity. The word 'holy' on its own means 'holy'. 'Holy, holy' means 'holier' and 'holy, holy, holy' (which is what the seraphim sing in Isaiah 6:3) means 'holiest'. So 'I will betroth you ... I will betroth you ... I will betroth you' may have the sense of 'most married'. 'You will be most married.' Certainly when you recognise how God completes each of these three promises, it is clear that He intends this to be a marriage that will last:

I will betroth you to me:
* for ever
* in righteousness and in justice, in steadfast love and in mercy
* in faithfulness

This section ends with the promise **You will know the LORD**. 'Know' in the Bible is the language of marital intimacy. So 'knowing' in the Bible is a metaphor for sex. Genesis 4:1, for example, says, 'Now Adam knew Eve his wife, and she conceived and bore Cain.' This is not because the writers were coy, but because sex really is an act of disclosure. Here, of course, God is not talking about physical intimacy, but that to which physical intimacy points: a deep relationship with God in which we know God and are known by God. In verse 8, Israel did not 'know' it was Yahweh who blessed her. In verse 13, she 'forgot' Him as she pursued other loves. But now she will 'know' Him.

A renewed home (2:18, 21-23)

> [18]'In that day I will make a covenant for them with the beasts of the field, the birds in the sky and the creatures that move along the ground. Bow and sword and battle I will abolish from the land, so that all may lie down in safety … (NIV)
>
> [21]'And in that day I will answer, declares the LORD,
> I will answer the heavens,
> and they shall answer the earth,
> [22] and the earth shall answer the grain, the wine, and the oil,
> and they shall answer Jezreel,
> [23]and I will sow her for myself in the land.
> And I will have mercy on No Mercy,
> and I will say to Not My People, "You are my people";
> and he shall say, "You are my God."'

One of the exciting things about getting married is setting up home together. So it had been for Israel. After God entered into a covenant relationship with them at Sinai, He gave them the land of Canaan.

Now a renewed marriage will lead to a renewed home. In verse 18, God makes a covenant with creation to create a secure home for His people. The language of beasts, birds and creeping things recalls God's gift of food in Genesis 1:30: '"And to every beast of the earth and to every bird of the heavens and to everything that creeps on the earth, everything that has the breath of life, I have given every green plant for food." And it was so.' Once again God will create a land of plenty with provision for every creature. It suggests a resumption of the harmony of Eden before the curse of Genesis 3. The language of a covenant with animals also recalls the story of Noah. God destroyed the earth with a flood, but saved Noah, his family and two of every kind of animal in an ark. After they leave the ark, God makes a covenant not just with Noah, but with the animals: 'Behold, I establish my covenant with you and your offspring after you, and with every living creature that is with you, the birds, the livestock, and every beast of the earth with you, as many as came out of the ark; it is for every beast of the earth' (Gen. 9:9-10). Just as Noah represented a new beginning after judgment with the promise of protection, so Israel is being promised a new beginning after judgment.

We have the same idea in verses 21-22. The **answering** is all as it should be. This is how the world was made to work. God answers the heavens by sending rain. The heavens answer the earth's needs for water. The earth answers the needs of the crops by channelling the water into the harvest. God will reverse the judgment of verse 9 where He took away Israel's grain and wine. The skies and land will respond to God so there is abundance. In chapter 1, **Jezreel** was a sign of judgment because of its association with bloodshed. But the word 'Jezreel' actually means 'God plants'. So now judgment is reversed as Jezreel becomes a sign of God's blessing.

We find the same pattern of reversal in verses 22-23 where we have three reversals. First, God will have mercy on those once called No-Mercy. Second, God will say 'You are my people' to those once called Not-My-People. Third, God's people will say 'You are my God.' With the final reversal, we are not told what the old situation was. But that is the point. They will say 'You are my God' where once they did not say 'You are my God' – where once they said nothing.

In that day

Three times in this section Hosea says **in that day** (2:16, 18, 21 or 'on that day' in verse 18 in the ESV). Hosea looks forward to what God will do through Jesus. The renewal of the earth will take place when Jesus returns in the future to create 'a home of righteousness' for His people (2 Pet.3:13). But the renewed marriage has already begun:

- Hosea 2:23 says: And I will have mercy on No Mercy, and I will say to Not My People, 'You are my people'; and he shall say, 'You are my God.'

- 1 Peter 2:10 says: 'Once you were not a people, but now you are God's people; once you had not received mercy, but now you have received mercy.'

Love an adulteress (3:1)

And the LORD said to me, 'Go again, love a woman who is loved by another man and is an adulteress, even as the LORD loves the children of Israel, though they turn to other gods and love cakes of raisins.'

In chapter 3, the action switches back to Hosea's relationship with Gomer. But God's relationship with His people is never far away because Hosea is to love Gomer **as the LORD loves the children of Israel** (3:1). Hosea is to enact and illustrate God's grace. Chapter 2 is the commentary on or explanation of the actions of chapter 3. Or rather, chapter 3 is an enacted parable that illustrates the message of chapter 2. Hosea's love for Gomer, despite her infidelity, mirrors God's love for His people despite their infidelity.

Loved by another man is literally 'loved by a friend'. The term 'friend' need not imply one of Hosea's friends. The point is more that the man with whom she is in a relationship is a friend rather than a husband. 'Boyfriend' or 'partner', we might say today.

Hosea was told to marry Gomer back in 1:2: 'When the LORD first spoke through Hosea, the LORD said to Hosea, "Go, take to yourself a wife of whoredom and have children of whoredom, for the land commits great whoredom by forsaking the LORD."' Was Gomer already promiscuous when Hosea married her? Or did she have an as yet unrealised tendency towards promiscuity? Was it that she was a normal woman from a prostituted nation? Or was she herself a prostitute? Or maybe even a shrine prostitute? A number of options have been suggested:

1. Gomer is currently chaste. But she will turn out to be adulterous and the children in 1:2 refer to the children she will have. 'Take a women who will be unchaste and build a family with her.' This is the view of the commentators Francis I. Andersen and David Noel Freedman,[3] and David Allan Hubbard.[4]

2. Gomer is chaste (before her marriage and before the events of chapter 3), but is called a wife of fornication because she is from Israel, the land of fornication. This is the view of Douglas Stuart.[5]

---

3.   Francis I. Andersen and David Noel Freedman, *Hosea*, Anchor Bible, Doubleday, 1980, 163-7.

4.   David Allan Hubbard, *Hosea*, TOTC, IVP, 1989, 54-5.

5.   Stuart, *Hosea-Jonah*, 27.

3. Gomer is currently unchaste, perhaps even a commercial prostitute. This is the view of Derek Kidner[6] and Duane Garrett.[7]

4. Gomer is currently unchaste and already has bastard children whom Hosea adopts. The children in 1:3-9 are subsequent children, at least the first of whom is born to Hosea. This is the view of Thomas Edward McComiskey.[8]

5. Gomer is not a practising prostitute in the commercial sense, but has taken part in the ritual sex that was part of the Baal religion. This is the view of Hans Walter Wolff[9] and James Luther Mays.[10]

6. The whole episode is a vision. This is the view of John Calvin.[11]

There was cultic prostitution at that time. Sex was part of Baal worship. People had sex with strangers to symbolise or evoke fertility. So a wife of prostitution may refer to a woman who had offered her body in a religious act rather than to a professional prostitute. Hosea talks about cultic prostitution in 4:14: 'the men themselves go aside with prostitutes and sacrifice with cult prostitutes.' But there Hosea uses a different Hebrew word to describe those who take part. Moreover, by the time we get to chapter 3, Gomer is living with another man. Even if she had only taken part in cultic sex when Hosea married her, she goes on to leave him to live with her lover, an act outside the scope of temple prostitution.

It is all too much for some commentators. The marginal comments of the 1599 Geneva Bible say of verse 2: 'That is, one that has been a harlot for a long time: not that the Prophet did this thing in effect, but he saw this in a vision, or else was commanded by God to set forth under this parable or figure the idolatry of the Synagogue, and of the people her

---

6.   Derek Kidner, *The Message of Hosea*, BST, IVP, 1981, 18-19.

7.   Garrett, *Hosea, Joel*, 43-54.

8.   McComiskey, 'Hosea' in *The Minor Prophets*, 12.

9.   Wolff, *Hosea*, 12-16.

10.   James Luther Mays, *Hosea*, OTL, SCM, 1969, 25-6.

11.   Calvin, *Commentaries on the Twelve Minor Prophets Vol. 1*, 44.

children.' In other words, it was all just a dream. Calvin also argues that this was a vision because marrying a promiscuous wife and accepting children born through promiscuity was unthinkable.

But there is no mention of a vision. The story is told as fact. Gomer is named, as is her father. We are also told about the weaning of her second child in 1:8. These are the kind of details that indicate a historical narrative rather than a visionary metaphor.

Calvin says, 'And yet it seems not consistent with reason, that the Lord should thus gratuitously render his Prophet contemptible; for how could he expect to be received on coming abroad before the public, after having brought on himself such a disgrace?' 'This, we know, was not done,' says Calvin.[12]

But this is the point. It was not done, but the LORD has done it. It is contemptible, but the LORD has opened Himself up to contempt. It is a disgrace, but the LORD has brought disgrace on Himself by making a covenant with faithless Israel. This act, which supposedly renders Hosea unqualified to be a prophet, is the very act that qualifies him to speak on the LORD's behalf. One cuckold speaks on behalf of another.

The Bible had already spoken of covenant unfaithfulness as an act of prostitution and promiscuity:

> 'You shall tear down their altars and break their pillars and cut down their Asherim (for you shall worship no other god, for the LORD, whose name is Jealous, is a jealous God), lest you make a covenant with the inhabitants of the land, and when they whore after their gods and sacrifice to their gods and you are invited, you eat of his sacrifice, and you take of their daughters for your sons, and their daughters whore after their gods and make your sons whore after their gods' (Exod. 34:13-16).

> And the LORD said to Moses, 'Behold, you are about to lie down with your fathers. Then this people will rise and whore after the foreign gods among them in the land that they are entering, and they will forsake me and break my covenant that I have made with them' (Deut. 31:16).

12. Calvin, *Commentaries on the Twelve Minor Prophets Vol. 1*, 44.

People may well have questioned Hosea. But each question was an opportunity to speak the word of the LORD. People may have disapproved of Hosea. But each time their disapproval rebounded on them. Their judgment against Hosea was a judgment against themselves and their own spiritual whoring.

Perhaps it rebounds on us. We may look disapprovingly at prostitution and adultery. But our disapproval rebounds on us. Which is worse? To be unfaithful towards another human being or to be unfaithful towards God? Neither is good, but infidelity towards God is worse.

The verse ends with a strange reference to raisin cakes. **The children of Israel ... turn to other gods and love cakes of raisins**. In the midst of the heartbreak caused by infidelity, why start talking about cakes? Raisin cakes were probably offered to Baal and then eaten by the worshippers to make them fertile. It seems a ridiculous thing to highlight. But perhaps that is the point. Imagine a churchgoer opting for a heretical church over an evangelical church because they serve doughnuts after the meeting. That is what the Israelites are doing. They prefer Baal to the LORD because Baal serves better cakes, ignoring the fact that the LORD provides their grain, their wine, their oil, their silver, their gold (2:8).

Bought with a price (3:2-3)

> [2]So I bought her for fifteen shekels of silver and a homer and a lethech of barley. [3]And I said to her, 'You must dwell as mine for many days. You shall not play the whore, or belong to another man; so will I also be to you.'

Hosea enacts God's love. But his actions also show us that a price must be paid for this relationship to be restored. Probably Gomer's indebtedness had reduced her to a state of slavery. She may have been sold by her creditor as a concubine. Whatever her circumstances, Hosea has to redeem her.

The **many days** may refer to a period of restoration designed to bring Gomer to repentance and renewed love. If so, it would parallel verses 4-5 which speak of God exiling Israel until they **return and seek the LORD their God** (3:5). The words **live** or 'dwell ... for many days' are repeated in verses 3 and 4 to describe first Gomer and then Israel. It reinforces the parallel between Gomer and Israel.

Hosea is to love her (3:1), redeem her (3:2) and restore her (3:3). Remember Hosea's actions are a living illustration of God's love for His people. This is the pattern for our redemption. God loves us. God redeems us. God restores us.

It cost Hosea to redeem Gomer. No doubt it cost him a good deal of emotional turmoil and angst. But there was also a price to pay: **fifteen shekels of silver and a homer and a lethech of barley** (3:2). And it cost God to redeem us. 1 Peter 1:18-19 says: 'For you know that it was not with perishable things such as silver or gold that you were redeemed from the empty way of life handed down to you from your forefathers, but with the precious blood of Christ, a lamb without blemish or defect.'

I am Gomer

We must not miss the point of Hosea's experience. It is to illustrate what God experiences in His relationship with Israel. The point of Hosea's story is for us to empathise with him. Imagine marrying, as Hosea does in chapter 1, a woman you know will abuse your love and betray you. And then imagine being asked, as Hosea is in 3:1, to forgive her betrayal. And then imagine having to pay, as Hosea has to in 3:2, to restore her. Perhaps today the equivalent might be posting bail or paying off accumulated debts. And then imagine bringing her into your home as Hosea does in 3:3. There is no indication in the story that Gomer is repentant. Perhaps Hosea must love her in the face of continued hostility in the hope of winning her love again.

We are invited to share Hosea's pain. But the point is that this is God's pain. And *we are Gomer*. The way Gomer treated Hosea is the way we have treated God. And what is God's response?

- He shows us His love again (3:1).

- He buys us back at the price of His Son's blood (3:2).

- He restores us to His presence (3:3).

Return (3:4-5)

[4]For the children of Israel shall dwell many days without king or prince, without sacrifice or pillar, without ephod or household gods. [5]Afterwards the children of Israel shall return and seek the LORD their God, and David their king, and they shall come in fear to the LORD and to his goodness in the latter days.

Verse 4 is a description of the exile when all the institutions of Israel (both the good and the bad) will be stripped away. The **pillar** was a sacred standing stone. The **ephod** was a waistcoat worn by a priest. It was part of the temple worship. But other ephods probably were being used in local idolatrous shrines and the ephod could also itself become an object of worship (Judg. 8:24-27).

Verse 4 describes going away into exile. Verse 5 describes return after exile. But this is so much more than a return from exile to the land. This is a return to God Himself. What is the link between returning to the land after exile and returning to God?

First, Israel did not go into exile because God forgot them or because the gods of Assyria and Babylon were stronger. They went into exile as an act of divine judgment. They went into exile because they had left God. In a sense, God exiled the people from the land because the people had exiled themselves from God.

Second, the exile of God's people in Assyria and Babylon was a picture of humanity's exile from God. Ever since Adam and Eve ate the fruit, we have been exiled from God's presence with the fiery sword of an angel barring our return (Gen. 3:24). God's judgment on Israel was a microcosm of His judgment on humanity. This means salvation is more than a return to the land. The final destination of God's saving purposes is a return to God Himself.

Hosea also says the children of Israel will return to **David their king**. But David is long dead. So this is not a return of the historical person David, but a return to a king in David's line. Hosea is talking about the new David whom God has promised would rescue God's people, and reign over them in peace and justice. Moreover, the Davidic king reigned in the southern kingdom of Judah whereas Hosea is ministering to the northern kingdom. So this verse suggests a new unified people.

Jesus is the One who ultimately ends this exile. Mark, for example, begins his Gospel quoting two prophecies predicting the end of the exile (Mark 1:1-3). His point is that Jesus is coming as the One who will bring the exile to an end. Jesus is God's promised king, the new David, who leads us home to God.

The latter days began with the cross and resurrection. They are the days between the first and second coming of Jesus, the days in which we live. We see verse 5 being fulfilled through the mission of the church as, through the proclamation of Jesus, God's true people **come in fear to the LORD and to his goodness**.

STUDY QUESTIONS

1. What is 'the logic of divine grace'?

2. Tim Keller says, 'Jesus is the only Lord who, if you receive him, will fulfil you completely, and, if you fail him, will forgive you eternally.'[13] Give examples of how other 'lords' do not fulfil us if we receive them.

3. Give examples of how other 'lords' do not forgive us if we fail them.

4. Reconstruct the story of Hosea's marriage.

5. How are we like Gomer?

6. How is Jesus like Hosea?

Questions for Personal Reflection

1. Do you think of Jesus as 'My Boss' or 'My Husband'?

2. Do you look on prostitutes with disdain? How might your disdain rebound on you?

3. Reread 2:14-23 as a message from God to you. Hear Him 'speak tenderly' to your heart (2:14).

---

13.   Keller, *The Reason for God*, 173.

4

God Presents His Case
(Hosea 4:1–5:7)

The opening verses of Hosea 4 are like a court summons. **The LORD has a charge to bring against you who live in the land** (4:1, NIV). Hosea started in the maternity ward with the naming of his children in chapter 1. Then we moved to the wilderness and the lovers' tryst. Then to the slave market as Hosea buys back Gomer. Now we come to the law court. But it is not that this is the next event in the story. We do not hear anything more about Hosea and Gomer. But the pattern exemplified in their marriage is the foundation of all that follows. Indeed, the word **controversy** in 4:1 is related to the word **plead** in 2:2. The case God pleaded in chapter 2 is now brought into the law court.

A broken marriage (4:1)

Hear the word of the LORD, O children of Israel, for the LORD has a controversy with the inhabitants of the land. There is no faithfulness or steadfast love, and no knowledge of God in the land.

A marriage is a legal agreement that requires faithfulness. But it is much more 'than a contract. **Steadfast love** is the commitment to the *spirit* of the marriage relationship as well as the *letter* of marriage vows. God's people were not being true to the letter of their covenantal relationship, nor to its spirit. They did not keep or acknowledge their obligations to God, nor did they love Him.

Hear the word of the LORD, you Israelites could simply be a summons to listen to what Hosea is about to say. But it could also have the meaning of *heed* the word that God has spoken. As we shall see, verse 2 echoes the Ten Commandments. So verse 1 could be a call to live by the word God gave His people at Mount Sinai.

God has a threefold accusation against His people: **There is no faithfulness, no love, no acknowledgment of God in the land (NIV).**

1. No faithfulness
Faithfulness or truth or integrity involves being true to your word and responsibilities. Without faithfulness the bonds between people are weakened and society becomes unstable. In contrast, God's promise in 2:20 is 'I will betroth you to me in faithfulness.'

2. No love
This is the term for covenant commitment or steadfast love. In other words, it refers to both affection and commitment. This is the marital love – a love that includes genuine affection, but which is also sustained by fidelity to covenantal promises. Perhaps you consider yourself a faithful member of your church, someone who is true to your obligations towards God. But do you love Him?

3. No knowledge
This knowledge is more than mere cognition. It is acknowledgment or a recognition of our obligations to another. The word was used in the Ancient Near East to denote recognition of an overlord's rights.

They are all relational terms. They are marriage terms. They are covenant terms. You can readily imagine a distraught wife or husband saying, 'He's not faithful to me.' 'She doesn't love me.' 'He doesn't know me, he doesn't understand me.'

A broken family (4:2)

> There is swearing, lying, murder, stealing, and committing adultery; they break all bounds, and bloodshed follows bloodshed.

If people are not committed to the spirit of their covenant with God, then they soon stop keeping the letter of the covenant. When Adam and Eve broke faith with God in Genesis 3, the result was murder in their family in Genesis 4. In the same way, the failure described in verse 1 of Israel's relationship to God means that the social breakdown described in verse 2 soon follows.

Five representative sins are listed which stand as examples of Israel's lawbreaking. Cursing is swearing, that is, making an oath using the LORD's name or evoking the LORD's name to call down calamity on another person. In other words, it involves a failure to keep the third commandment: 'You shall not take the name of the LORD your God in vain, for the LORD will not hold him guiltless who takes his name in vain.' (Exod. 20:7) So all these crimes are clear violations of the Ten Commandments. To curse, lie, murder, steal and commit adultery are to break the third, ninth, sixth, eighth and seventh of the Ten Commandments. The result is a breakdown of family and society.

A broken home (4:3)

Therefore the land mourns, and all who dwell in it languish, and also the beasts of the field and the birds of the heavens, and even the fish of the sea are taken away.

Twice already in verse 1 God has said **in the land**. God's charge is **against you who live in the land**. This reference to the land reminds us that the Israelites' possession of the land was under the terms of the covenant. The covenant made through Moses included blessings for obedience and curses for disobedience. And central to those curses was exile from the land, though they also included drought (Deut. 28:22-24; Lev. 26:19). The people had broken their tenancy agreement, as it were, and now their tenancy was in jeopardy. The repetition of **in the land** at the end of verse 1 repeats this idea of God's redemptive gift and its corresponding obligations.

Now in verse 3 God's judgment is said to affect the land. The land is personified and said to be in mourning. The history of humanity is replayed in the history of Israel. Adam was given a beautiful world to care for and God blessed that world. But

Adam rebelled against God and, as a result, the world was subject to humanity's misrule and God's curse. In the same way, Israel was given a beautiful land to care for, a land flowing with milk and honey through God's blessing. But Israel rebelled against God and, as result, the land is becoming subject to Israel's misrule and God's curse. A repetition of the Fall is taking place. Humanity was appointed as rulers over creation. Our failure in that role leads to the return of chaos to the earth. Humanity was made to rule over creation, but now our rule is corrupt so creation is subject to frustration. Israel were redeemed to rule over the land of Canaan. But now they, too, were failing and the land was suffering. Hosea 4:3 says the land **mourns**. Perhaps Paul had this in mind when he wrote Romans 8 because the word that the Septuagint, the Greek version of the Old Testament, uses to translate 'mourns' is the same word Paul uses in Romans 8 when he describes the way creation 'groans':

> For the creation was subjected to futility, not willingly, but because of him who subjected it, in hope that the creation itself will be set free from its bondage to decay and obtain the freedom of the glory of the children of God. We know that the whole creation has been *groaning* as in the pains of childbirth right up to the present time. (Rom. 8:20-22)

Verse 3 echoes the three categories of creature (beasts, birds and fish) highlighted in Genesis 1:20, 24, 28 over which humanity was to rule. Now, however, the blessings of Genesis 1 have become curses and the rule of humanity has become a threat. The emphatic **even** in verse 3 (*even* **the fish of the sea are taken away**) suggests a judgment even greater than that of Noah's flood. The flood of Genesis 6–9 destroyed the birds and beasts except for the few saved in the ark. But the sea creatures were obviously spared. However, God's coming judgment will affect *even* the fish.

Our broken marriage (4:1) leads to a broken human family (4:2) and a broken home (4:3). But there is hope. The promise in 2:16-23 that God's marriage with His people would be restored included within it the promise of a restored home. 'And I will make for them a covenant on that day with the beasts of the field, the birds of the heavens, and the creeping things of the ground. And I will abolish the bow, the sword, and war from the land, and I will make you lie down in safety.' (2:18)

Failing clergy (4:4-9)

In Hosea 4:1, God has charged His people with no faithfulness, no love and no knowledge. The following chapters pick up on these three accusations. Chapter 4 focuses on 'no knowledge' or 'no acknowledgment'. It is not just a lack of information. Knowing God is more relational than that. If I say, 'I know about the Queen', then I am claiming to be able to recall some information about her. But if I claim that 'I know the Queen', I am implying a personal relationship with her. So by 'no knowledge' Hosea means 'no relationship' with God.

> [4]Yet let no one contend,
>   and let none accuse,
>   for with you is my contention, O priest.
> [5]You shall stumble by day;
>   the prophet also shall stumble with you by night;
>   and I will destroy your mother.
> [6]My people are destroyed for lack of knowledge;
>   because you have rejected knowledge,
>   I reject you from being a priest to me.
> And since you have forgotten the law of your God,
>   I also will forget your children.
> [7]The more they increased,
>   the more they sinned against me;
>   I will change their glory into shame.
> [8]They feed on the sin of my people;
>   they are greedy for their iniquity.
> [9]And it shall be like people, like priest;
>   I will punish them for their ways
>   and repay them for their deeds.

Verse 4 is difficult to translate because the original text is unclear. It could be a call not to accuse the priests as the NIV suggests: **your people are like those who bring charges against a priest**. The problem with this is that verse 6 is itself an accusation against the priests and verse 9 suggests the priests may be hypocritically accusing the people. So the context suggests the ESV is correct: **Yet let no one contend, and let none accuse, for with you is my contention, O priest**.

'Too right', you can imagine a religious person saying. 'You tell them, Hosea.' The word **contention** in verse 4 is the same as the word 'controversy' in verse 1. We should imagine the priests hearing God's accusation in verses 1-3 and nodding in agreement. Following the opening accusation of verses 1-3, perhaps we should think of these words as the defence case, if not for all the people then at least for their religious elite. But God says the priests are no different from the people. **It shall be like people, like priest; I will punish them for their ways and repay them for their deeds'** (4:9).

Chapter 4 contains three accusations and three announcements of judgment:

verses 1-2	an accusation against the inhabitants of the land
verse 3	a declaration of judgment against the land
verse 4	an accusation against the priests
verses 5-9	a declaration of judgment against the priests
verses 10-18	an accusation against the people
verse 19	a declaration of judgment against the people

Hosea is saying to the priests, 'Don't accuse other people because you are no different.' Hosea's message to the religious people of his day is echoed by Jesus in the Sermon on the Mount:

Judge not, that you be not judged. For with the judgment you pronounce you will be judged, and with the measure you use it will be measured to you. Why do you see the speck that is in your brother's eye, but do not notice the log that is in your own eye? Or how can you say to your brother, "Let me take the speck out of your eye," when there is the log in your own eye? You hypocrite, first take the log out of your own eye, and then you will see clearly to take the speck out of your brother's eye. (Matt. 7:1-5)

Elsewhere the New Testament calls on us to 'speak the truth in love' to one another (Eph. 4:15), and to rebuke one another and lead our brothers and sisters away from sin (Gal. 6:1-3). But here we are told not to judge. Does this mean we cannot do pastoral care until we have sorted out sin in our own lives? Because if it does mean that, then we will never do it!

The key is the word 'hypocrite'. The person who tries to remove the speck is a hypocrite. The hypocrite in the Sermon on the Mount is a self-righteous person who does what he does to be seen by men and to establish his own righteousness (6:2, 5, 16). If you do not pastor people out of a strong sense of God's grace – both to you and to them – then you will leave them feeling condemned. And there is no condemnation to those who are in Christ Jesus (Rom. 8:1). If you leave people feeling condemned, then something has gone horribly wrong in your pastoral care. Self-righteous people make bad pastors. At best, they create legalists in their own image; at worst, they leave people crushed and condemned.

Hosea's words are also echoed by Paul in Romans 2:1-5:

> Therefore you have no excuse, O man, every one of you who judges. For in passing judgment on another you condemn yourself, because you, the judge, practise the very same things. We know that the judgment of God rightly falls on those who do such things. Do you suppose, O man – you who judge those who do such things and yet do them yourself – that you will escape the judgment of God? Or do you presume on the riches of his kindness and forbearance and patience, not knowing that God's kindness is meant to lead you to repentance? But because of your hard and impenitent heart you are storing up wrath for yourself on the day of wrath when God's righteous judgment will be revealed.

In Romans 1, Paul has exposed humanity's sin, sin that starts with exchanging 'the truth about God for a lie' and worshipping 'the creature rather than the Creator' (Rom. 1:24-25) and comes to fruition in all kinds of evil (Rom. 1:26-32).

'Hear, hear,' the moral person says. 'Those dreadful pagans!' 'But you, too, will be judged,' says Paul. God's wrath is being stored up like a dam, waiting to burst upon you. God will not judge our respectable exteriors, but our rebellious hearts and our dark secrets. He is going to look into our hearts – blatantly evil people and morally respectable people alike. And he is going to expose our secrets. He is going to judge the desire in all of us to be god of our own lives. 'I lived a good life,' will be no excuse because it will not stand up in the court. The evidence will not support it.

The priests in Hosea's day should have taught the people the knowledge of God and encouraged them to know God. But they have rejected the knowledge of God, so God will reject them (4:6). As in chapter 2, Israel is portrayed as a mother while individuals Israelites are her children. It is as if we are witnessing a divorce case as a result of which the children suffer. Because both priests and prophets have failed to teach the knowledge of God, Mother Israel will be judged: **You [priests] shall stumble by day; the prophet also shall stumble with you by night; and I will destroy your mother** (4:5). Hosea then says, **My people are destroyed for lack of knowledge** (4:6). The destruction of Mother Israel inevitably means the destruction of her children.

There is a double pronouncement of judgment in which the punishment fits the crime: **Because you have rejected knowledge, I reject you from being a priest to me. And since you have forgotten the law of your God, I also will forget your children** (4:6). The priesthood was hereditary, so the forgetting **your children** could be the children of the priests. If they were forgotten, then the priesthood would be rejected. But elsewhere in Hosea 'your children' are individual Israelites so it may not be the physical offspring of the priests, but the children of Mother Israel. The failure of the priests impacts on the whole nation, who are themselves complicit in their failure to acknowledge God.

The pride of Israel in 5:5 (ESV) is God Himself (not 'Israel's arrogance' as the NIV translates it). God should have been their pride and joy. God should have been their source of status and reputation. But now God withdraws and so **I will change their glory into shame** (4:7). In 1 Samuel 15:29, the phrase 'the Glory of Israel' is used as a name of God Himself. Israel's glory is her knowledge of God. But now she has rejected that knowledge. Jeremiah 2:11 says: 'Has a nation changed its gods, even though they are no gods? But my people have changed their glory for that which does not profit.' Paul expands on this idea in Romans 1. Humanity's fundamental problem is a double exchange:

- We have 'exchanged the glory of the immortal God for images resembling mortal man and birds and animals and reptiles.' (Rom. 1:23) In other words, we do not worship God.

- We have 'exchanged the truth about God for a lie.' (Rom. 1:25) In other words, we so not trust God.

As a result, God gives us over to our 'sinful desires,' 'shameful lusts' and 'a depraved mind' (Rom. 1:24, 26, 28). Our shameful behaviour stems from that double exchange: we 'exchanged the truth of God for a lie, and worshipped and served created things rather than the Creator' (Rom. 1:25).

They feed on the sin of my people in verse 8 is a pun. The word for 'sin' is also the word for 'sin offering'. The priests had a right to a portion of sacrificed animals (Lev. 7:28-38). It may be the priests were rejoicing in the people's sins because it meant more business or they may have been abusing the system (as happened in 1 Sam. 2:12-17). It is not hard to think of businesses today that feed on people's sin. One readily thinks of the sex industry and the drugs trade, but it may be that other more legitimate businesses also depend on people's greed and gluttony.

We need to pray that our church leaders develop a deep, personal knowledge of God and that they might faithfully proclaim the knowledge of God to us. We cannot rest on our heritage. Rejoice in the traditions of your church or denomination by all means. They are a great asset. But do not put your trust in them. We need to live with a fresh experience of God in and through His Word. We need our own knowledge of God. We need to hide God's Word in our hearts.

Verse 9 says **like people, like priests**. Church leaders and church members can collude in a lack of knowledge. The people do not want to be challenged and the people's leaders do not want the unpopularity that challenging people brings. 2 Timothy 4:3-4 says: 'For the time is coming when people will not endure sound teaching, but having itching ears they will accumulate for themselves teachers to suit their own passions, and will turn away from listening to the truth and wander off into myths.' So think about how you can contribute to a church culture that supports the faithful teaching of God's Word.

Citing Hosea 4, the Puritan John Flavel warns us not to despise the knowledge of Christ as the people in Hosea's day did. He highlights three ways we can do this:

- treating it lightly
- ignoring its directions
- failing to know more of Christ

To the people that sit under the doctrine of Christ daily, and have the light of his knowledge shining round about them: Take heed ye do not reject and despise this light. *Firstly,* when you despise the means of knowledge by slight and low esteem of it ... *Secondly,* you despise the knowledge of Christ, when you despise the directions and loving constraints of that knowledge; when you refuse to be guided by your knowledge, your light and your lusts contest and struggle within you. [*Thirdly,*] take heed that you rest not satisfied with that knowledge of Christ you have attained, but grow on towards perfection ... And it is the sin, even of the best of saints, when they see how deep the knowledge of Christ lies, and what pains they must take to dig for it, to throw by the shovel of duty, and cry, *Dig we cannot.* To your work, Christians, to your work.

With these exhortations, Flavel gives this warning:

Surely, if you thus reject knowledge, God will reject you for it, Hosea 4:6. It is a despising of the richest gift that ever Christ gave to the church; and however it be a contempt and slight that begins low ... yet believe it, it is daring sin that flies higher than you are aware, Luke 10:16. "He that despiseth you, despiseth me; and he that despiseth me, despiseth him that sent me."[1]

Failing worship (4:10-19)

[10]They shall eat, but not be satisfied;
    they shall play the whore, but not multiply,
because they have forsaken the LORD
    to cherish [11]whoredom, wine, and new wine,
    which take away the understanding.
[12]My people inquire of a piece of wood,
    and their walking staff gives them oracles.
For a spirit of whoredom has led them astray,
    and they have left their God to play the whore.
[13]They sacrifice on the tops of the mountains

---

1.   John Flavel, 'The Fountain of Life,' *Works Volume 1*, Banner of Truth, 1820, 1968, 41-2.

and burn offerings on the hills,
under oak, poplar, and terebinth,
   because their shade is good.
Therefore your daughters play the whore,
   and your brides commit adultery.
[14]I will not punish your daughters when they play the whore,
   nor your brides when they commit adultery;
for the men themselves go aside with prostitutes
   and sacrifice with cult prostitutes,
and a people without understanding shall come to ruin.
[15]Though you play the whore, O Israel,
   let not Judah become guilty.
Enter not into Gilgal, nor go up to Beth-aven,
   and swear not, 'As the LORD lives.'
[16]Like a stubborn heifer,
   Israel is stubborn;
can the LORD now feed them
   like a lamb in a broad pasture?
[17]Ephraim is joined to idols;
   leave him alone.
[18]When their drink is gone, they give themselves to whoring;
   their rulers dearly love shame.
[19]A wind has wrapped them in its wings,
   and they shall be ashamed because of their sacrifices.

This section opens with Hosea's accusation against the priests. They have failed to teach the people the knowledge of God. It is difficult to know where Hosea's message moves away from a focus on the priests and broadens out to address the people. But perhaps that is the point. **Like people, like priest**, Hosea says in 4:9. There is not much difference between them. They are both as bad as each other.

The result is described in verses 14-19: the people commit immorality. And they do so both literally and metaphorically. Twice Hosea says the daughters of Israel **play the whore** and her brides **commit adultery** (13, 14). This may be a picture of Israel's idolatry. But they are linked to the description of the nation's men who **go aside with prostitutes and sacrifice with cult prostitutes** (14), which would appear to be a literal description. Yet the passage certainly contains figurative descriptions of Israel's spiritual adultery. **They have left their God to play the whore** (12). **'Ephraim is joined to idols'** (17).

Ephraim was the most important tribe in the northern kingdom of Israel and often the term was used to represent Israel as a whole. The word **'joined'** here is a covenantal term. So it has the sense of 'Israel is wedded to idols.' Israel as a whole has played the whore (15). So the likely scenario is that Hosea is describing the spiritual adultery of the nation as a whole that has **left their God** to run after other gods. But the Baal cult involved ritual prostitution in which worshippers acted out the fertility sought from the gods with shrine prostitutes. So the nation's figurative adultery involved her in literal adultery.

We know that adultery is wrong and we readily judge adulterous people. But we, too, have failed to be faithful to God. And adultery towards God is surely worse than adultery towards other people. Our self-righteous condemnation of others will rebound on us.

In 4:15 God says: **Though you play the whore, O Israel, let not Judah become guilty. Enter not into Gilgal, nor go up to Beth-aven, and swear not, "As the LORD lives."** God turns from addressing the northern kingdom of Israel to address the southern kingdom of Judah. And what He says, in effect, is, 'If you visit Israel, don't go to church because God isn't there.' **Beth-aven** in 4:15 and 5:8 is almost certainly a pun. It probably referred to Bethel. Bethel means 'house of God', but Bethel is no longer a house of God. Now it is Beth-aven, a 'house of wickedness'.

G. K. Chesterton is famously reported to have said, 'When we cease to worship God, we do not worship nothing, we worship anything.' And this is what was happening. Without the knowledge of God, the people are worshipping sacred trees (4:13) and engaging in ritual prostitution (4:14). The New Living Translation captures how ridiculous this is in its translation of 4:12: **They ask a piece of wood for advice! They think a stick can tell them the future!**

Does that sound ridiculous? Let me tell you what is ridiculous. This past week I spent 24 hours wallowing in self-pity because someone had not affirmed me in the way I wanted. It turns out the glory of God is not enough for me. I worship myself and make an idol of my reputation. And I crumble when that idol is threatened.

But idols do not provide. **They shall eat, but not be satisfied; they shall play the whore, but not multiply, because they have forsaken the LORD to cherish whoredom, wine, and new wine** (4:10-11). **When their drink is gone, they give themselves to whoring; their rulers dearly love shame** (4:18). There is more to God's judgment than dissatisfaction in this life. But it can certainly include this.

All the time God is ready to care for them like a shepherd. He is ready to **feed them like a lamb in a broad pasture** (4:16). But **the Israelites are stubborn, like a stubborn heifer** (4:16). The result will be:

Shame: **I will change their glory into shame** (4:7). **Their rulers dearly love shame ... and they shall be ashamed because of their sacrifices** (4:18-19).

Judgment: **I will punish them for their ways and repay them for their deeds** (4:9). **A wind has wrapped them in its wings, and they shall be ashamed because of their sacrifices** (4:19).

The word **wind** in verse 19 is the same as the word **spirit** in verse 12. **A spirit of whoredom has led them astray,** says verse 12. Perhaps at the time that spirit brought with it a sense of excitement. But now that spiritual promiscuity has wrapped itself around the people like a tornado and is sweeping them up into destruction.

For what are you living? What do you think about most? What is your big desire? How would you complete the sentence, 'I would be happy if ...' Your answer threatens to be an idol to you – unless your answer is God Himself.

The verdict (5:1-7)

Chapter 4 introduced a lawsuit that God was bringing against his people. Attention soon focused on the priests and their failure to lead people to the knowledge of God. Chapter 5 begins as chapter 4 did with a call to **hear** what God is saying. In chapter 4, God opened the court proceedings. Now He is declaring his verdict:

> [1]Hear this, O priests!
>   Pay attention, O house of Israel!
>   Give ear, O house of the king!
>   For the judgment is for you;

for you have been a snare at Mizpah
and a net spread upon Tabor.
²And the revolters have gone deep into slaughter,
but I will discipline all of them.
³I know Ephraim,
and Israel is not hidden from me;
for now, O Ephraim, you have played the whore;
Israel is defiled (5:1-3).

These verses repeat the accusation of chapter 4. The priests and politicians have been a snare to the people, leading them into rebellion against God. Their policies have led to slaughter (5:2) and corruption (5:3). Above all, they have turned to prostitution. This was Hosea's central accusation (1:2): God's people were serving other gods like an adulterous wife (5:7).

³I know Ephraim,
and Israel is not hidden from me;
for now, O Ephraim, you have played the whore;
Israel is defiled.
⁴Their deeds do not permit them
to return to their God.
For the spirit of whoredom is within them,
and they know not the LORD.
⁵The pride of Israel testifies to his face;
Israel and Ephraim shall stumble in his guilt;
Judah also shall stumble with them. (5:3-5)

Now God presents the evidence. In verse 3 God says that He knows all about Ephraim (another name of Israel). **Israel is not hidden from me**. We cannot hide what we do from God. He sees even our inner thoughts. **The pride of Israel** could be 'Israel's arrogance' which 'testifies against them', as the NIV suggests. In this sense, Israel's attitude in court, as it were, proves the case against them. They arrogantly refuse to return to God or acknowledge Him (5:4). But 'the pride of Israel' is, as we have noted, more likely to be God Himself. God has witnessed their sin (5:3) and now He Himself takes the stand to testifies against them (5:5).

²And the revolters have gone deep into slaughter,
but I will discipline all of them …
⁶With their flocks and herds they shall go

to seek the LORD,
but they will not find him;
  he has withdrawn from them.
7They have dealt faithlessly with the LORD;
  for they have borne alien children.
Now the new moon shall devour them with their fields.

Now the court case reaches its climax as the sentence is passed. God will discipline His people. And He will do so by withdrawing Himself from them. God disciplines them by giving them what they want. They think they can manage without acknowledging God (5:4). So God will let them see what life without His provision and protection is like.

The phrase **the pride of Israel testifies to his face** is repeated and in both cases it is linked to seeking the LORD. But in 5:5-6 the people seek God and in 7:10 they do not:

5The pride of Israel testifies to his face …
6With their flocks and herds they shall go
  to seek the LORD,
but they will not find him;
  he has withdrawn from them. (5:5-6)

10The pride of Israel testifies to his face;
  yet they do not return to the LORD their God,
  nor seek him, for all this. (7:10)

So do they seek God or not? The answer is that in chapter 5 they seek God **with their flocks and herds**. In other words, they seek Him by offering sacrifices – that is what the flocks are for. But it is mere religious formality. They do not really seek the LORD. They go through the motions, but there is no real love. In Hosea 6:6, God reminds us: 'For I desire steadfast love and not sacrifice, the knowledge of God rather than burnt offerings.' And Hosea 4:19 says: **they shall be ashamed because of their sacrifices**. In other words, their sacrifices are not a sign of the people's faith in God's provision. They are merely going through the motions. It is a hypocritical attempt to manipulate God. When and if the people come to their senses, they will look back on these religious performances with shame. It is a reminder to us of the dangers of mere formality in our approach to worship.

There is hope in the word **discipline** (5:2). It implies correction rather than final punishment. God is disciplining His people in love so that they will **return** and **acknowledge** Him (5:4).

Does God seem far away from you at the moment? Verse 4 says: **Their deeds do not permit them to return to their God. For the spirit of whoredom is within them, and they know not the LORD.** Could it be there is some sin of which you need to repent? Could it be your affections are divided? Could it be God wants you to acknowledge your need of Him?

STUDY QUESTIONS

1. God's accusation is 'no faithfulness or steadfast love, and no knowledge of God' (4:1). What signs of this do we see today in society?

2. What signs of this do we see today in the church?

3. Hosea 4:2 shows that a breakdown in our relationship with God leads to a breakdown in our relationship with one another. What signs of this do we see today?

4. Hosea 4:3 shows that a breakdown in our relationship with God leads to a breakdown in our relationship with creation. What signs of this do we see today?

5. What is the difference between hypocritical accusations (Hosea 4:4; Matt. 7:1-5) and speaking the truth in love (Eph. 4:15; Gal. 6:1-3)?

6. Hosea 4:9 says: 'Like people, like priest.' What positive examples can you identify of the connection between church leaders and the churches they lead?

7. What negative examples can you identify of the connection between church leaders and the churches they lead?

8. What do people in your context worship instead of God?

Questions for Personal Reflection

1. What do you worship instead of God? Think it through by asking yourself: For what are you living? What do you think about most? What is your big desire?

2. How would you complete the sentence, 'I would be happy if ...' If your answer is not God-centred then it may reveal your idolatrous desires.

3. As you pursue these idolatrous desires, what happens when things go wrong? How does this desire leave you feeling?

5

God Heals His People
(Hosea 5:8–6:3)

It is Easter morning and you are gathered as a church. What is the connection? Maybe that seems an obvious question. Surely there is no better time for Christians to gather to worship the Risen Christ than on Easter Sunday. But I want to suggest there is a much deeper connection. And if we grasp this connection it may transform our churches.

We often tell the Easter story along these lines: 'Christ died for me and then rose again to demonstrate that God has accepted the sacrifice that He made on my behalf.' That is gloriously true. But the resurrection is bigger than that. Christ rose to create, to heal, to restore *a people* – a people who will be His people. To see how this works, we need first to see how God *destroys* His people.

I will tear (5:8-15)
So far in Hosea we have moved from the maternity ward to the wilderness to the slave market and to the law court. Now we move to the battlefield. Chapter 4 opened with a court summons. Now 5:8 opens with a battle cry: **Blow the horn in Gibeah, the trumpet in Ramah. Sound the alarm at Beth-aven.**

In chapter 4, the court summons was brought. The accusation was made: 'There is no faithfulness or steadfast love, and no knowledge of God in the land' (4:1). The defence case was dismissed and the verdict was given. And what is the verdict of the court? 'When they go with their flocks and herds to seek the LORD, they will not find him; he has withdrawn himself from them' (5:6).

God will withdraw himself from them. I cannot convey how terrible those words are for God's people. God is their joy, their hope, their protection, their security, their provider, their rescuer, their pride. And now He is gone. Verses 8-15 describe what happens when God withdraws from us.

> [8]Blow the horn in Gibeah,
>   the trumpet in Ramah.
> Sound the alarm at Beth-aven;
>   we follow you, O Benjamin!
> [9]Ephraim shall become a desolation
>   in the day of punishment;
> among the tribes of Israel
>   I make known what is sure.
> [10]The princes of Judah have become
>   like those who move the landmark;
> upon them I will pour out
>   my wrath like water.
> [11]Ephraim is oppressed, crushed in judgment,
>   because he was determined to go after filth.

This section begins with an alarm call. **Sound the trumpet** (5:8, NIV). This is a call to man the ramparts for an invading army is coming. This is a call to sound the air-raid sirens. It is Hosea's dramatic way of warning of Assyrian invasion from the north. Because God has withdrawn, they must **blow the horn in Gibeah, the trumpet in Ramah** (5:8). Israel is left defenceless. And so **Ephraim is oppressed, crushed in judgment, because he was determined to go after filth** (5:11).

Gibeah and **Ramah** are border towns (5:8). You might expect them to be on the northern border of Israel, the direction from which the Assyrians would come. In fact, they are on the southern border. It is a sign that the Assyrians will penetrate deep into Israel and out the other side. The invading army will spread throughout the land. In verse 6, God in His judgment withdraws His protection and so now Israel is left defenceless.

At this point in their history God's people are divided into two: the northern kingdom of Israel or Ephraim and the southern kingdom of Judah. Most of Hosea's ministry is to the northern kingdom. But here he addresses the southern kingdom as well. Both kingdoms are threatened by Assyrian invasion. And so it proved. Israel was completely destroyed and Judah became a vassal state (2 Chron. 28:16-21).

Verse 10 says: **The princes of Judah have become like those who move the landmark; upon them I will pour out my wrath like water.** The accusation is that Judah is moving boundary stones. The implication is that they will try to take advantage of Israel's weakness by annexing its territory. But the references to Gibeah and Ramah in verse 8 are also a warning to Judah. These are towns near her borders. Judah cannot assume it will be safe with Israel acting as a kind of buffer between them and the Assyrian threat. The Assyrian army can readily reach as far down as Judah's border. Judah, too, must turn to the LORD in repentance or face the withdrawal of His protection from the Assyrian threat.

God withdrawing His protection is a terrible thing. Verses 8-11 are a warning that the Assyrians are coming. But something much worse is going to happen. Verses 12-14 are a warning that God Himself is coming.

> [12]But I am like a moth to Ephraim,
>   and like dry rot to the house of Judah.
> [13]When Ephraim saw his sickness,
>   and Judah his wound,
> then Ephraim went to Assyria,
>   and sent to the great king.
> But he is not able to cure you
>   or heal your wound.
> [14]For I will be like a lion to Ephraim,
>   and like a young lion to the house of Judah.
> I, even I, will tear and go away;
>   I will carry off, and no one shall rescue.

The background to verse 13 may well lie in the story of King Menahem. Pul, king of Assyria, invaded and Menahem bought the Assyrians off with a tribute of a thousand talents of silver. He raised this sum by taxing the people of Israel. All this happened during Hosea's lifetime. King Menahem, as it were, **went to Assyria** to heal **his sickness.** But the cure was short-lived. A few years later, Assyria would return to destroy Israel.

But there is something even worse that an Assyrian army coming against you and that is to have God come against you. A war against the Assyrians was a frightening prospect, especially if you no longer had God's protection. But a war against God Himself was truly terrifying. Yet that is what the Bible teaches.

God's righteous response involves not only His passive withdrawal, but His active judgment. **I, even I, will tear and go away; I will carry off** (5:14). There is a double emphasis:

- First, Israel will be torn by God and not by someone else. *I will tear*, says God. In other words, 'I myself will do this, not someone else' (even if in reality God uses someone else as His instrument of judgment). God is not just abandoning them to others. He Himself is going to do this.

- Second, Israel will be torn by God, even though He is her husband. *Even* I will tear, says God. 'Even though I am your husband, I will do this because of your covenant unfaithfulness.'

The New Testament describes us as enemies of God (Rom. 5:10; Phil. 3:18; James 4:4). We are at war with God. And in our battle against God there is only ever going to be one winner.

God's judgment is both passive and proactive. In this life it is often passive. 'God gave them up' or handed them over to wickedness, Paul says in Romans 1:24, 26, 28. God's gives us over to our sin by lifting His hand of restraint. People live with the consequences of their sin. Communities live with the consequences of sin. When there is no faithfulness, no love, no knowledge of God in the land (4:1), 'there is swearing, lying, murder, stealing, and committing adultery; they break all bounds, and bloodshed follows bloodshed. Therefore the land mourns, and all who dwell in it languish' (4:2-3). Our sin leads to all kinds of social ills because God passively judges us by letting our sin takes its course.

But God's judgment is also proactive. Hell is not just of our making. There is a sense in which that is true. We can create hell on earth through our sin. But the bigger truth is that God makes Hell (capital 'H'). Hell is God's eternal judgment on our sin. 'I, even I, will tear and go away.'

Hosea tries to capture the terror of this in a series of powerful images. He says God will be like:

- a flood of water (5:10)
- a devouring moth (5:12)
- corrosive rot (5:12)
- a festering wound (5:13)
- a vicious lion (5:14)

The Assyrian army might be what God uses, but God Himself is enacting judgment.

And when God tears you apart, no one can bind you up. **When Ephraim saw his sickness, and Judah his sores, then Ephraim turned to Assyria, and sent to the great king for help. But he is not able to cure you, not able to heal your sores** (5:13, NIV).

Verse 15 suggests there is hope: **I will return again to my place, until they acknowledge their guilt and seek my face, and in their distress earnestly seek me.** God is ready to return to His people. His withdrawal in 5:6 can be reversed. He will return to His people if they return to Him in repentance. But first He abandons them so that they will seek Him. In a sermon on this verse, Jonathan Edwards, the great American preacher and theologian, said:

> This is God's ordinary way before great and signal expressions of his mercy and favour. He very commonly so orders it in his providence, and so influences men by his Spirit, that they are brought to see their miserable condition as they are in themselves, and to despair of help from themselves, or from an arm of flesh, before he appears for them, and also makes them sensible of their sin, and their unworthiness of God's help.[1]

Edwards goes on to urge his hearers not to ignore or suppress any feelings of conviction of sin. This may be God's work in their lives to lead them to salvation. Instead, they should see

---

1.   Jonathan Edwards, 'Occasional Sermons: Sermon II, Hosea v.15,' *Works*, Ball, Arnold & Co., 1840, Volume 2, 830.

such conviction as God's prompting to run to Christ to find mercy.

The tragedy for the Israelites was that most of them did not heed this declaration of war. It is a tragedy repeated every time someone hears God's warning of judgment and ignores it.

I will heal (6:1-3)

In the middle of this court case, Hosea speaks and this is what he says:

> ¹Come, let us return to the LORD;
>> for he has torn us, that he may heal us;
>> he has struck us down, and he will bind us up.
> ²After two days he will revive us;
>> on the third day he will raise us up,
>> that we may live before him.
> ³Let us know; let us press on to know the LORD;
>> his going out is sure as the dawn;
> he will come to us as the showers,
>> as the spring rains that water the earth.

In chapters 4 and 5, we found ourselves in the courtroom facing the accusations of God. The evidence has been laid out and the verdict of judgment is certain. But suddenly there is a dramatic intervention. Hosea himself speaks. There is still hope. God has torn (5:14), but he will bind up. God has struck down, but he will heal.

> Come, let us return to the LORD;
>> for he has torn us, that he may heal us;
>> he has struck us down, and he will bind us up (6:1).

Maybe you are a Christian who is going through a difficult time. Maybe it is God's discipline, not to get back at you, but to lessen your attachment to the things of this world and increase your attachment to Him. Hosea's message to you is: Wait. *Wait for God the healer.* Wait for God in faith. Wait for Him to bind you up and revive you.

Or maybe you are going through a difficult time and you are not a follower of Jesus. This difficult experience may be God's wake-up call to you, God's invitation to you. Or maybe life for you is great. To you Hosea says **sound the alarm** because God is coming in judgment (5:8). He says: 'They do not realise that I remember all their evil deeds. Their sins engulf them; they are always before me.' (7:2 NIV) Hosea's message to you is this: Turn. **Come, let us return to the LORD** (6:1). *Turn to God the healer.*

But how can God be both the tearer and the healer? How can God tear up and at the same time heal those who turn to Him? How can He strike us down and at the same time bind up His people?

The answer is the cross of Jesus. There at the cross God tore us apart. Yet not us, but the One who stood in our place – Jesus, the representative of God's people. Jesus was torn that we might be healed. Jesus was struck down that we might be raised up. Jesus died the death we deserve so that we might live in God's presence.

The ESV translates 5:15 as: **I will return again to my place, until they acknowledge their guilt and seek my face, and in their distress earnestly seek me.** But the NIV translates it: **Then I will return to my lair until they have borne their guilt and seek my face – in their misery they will earnestly seek me.** At first sight, it appears to suggest that Israel will be punished, but when it has served its sentence God will return. But how can sinful people atone the wrath of a holy God? The answer is the cross. At the cross when Christ bore the guilt of our sin in our place.

When God wounds you, no one can heal you (5:13). But there is one glorious exception. God Himself can heal. And He heals you through His own wounds. 'He himself bore our sins in his body on the tree, that we might die to sin and live to righteousness. By his wounds you have been healed' (1 Pet. 2:24).

God is a strange enemy! One of the key rules of military tactics is the value of a surprise attack. But God warns of His coming. He calls for the horn to be blown and the alarm to be sounded. And then God provides a way of escape from His own coming.

> After two days he will revive us;
> > on the third day he will raise us up,
> > that we may live before him. (6:2)

Now this might remind you of something! It may well be verses like this that Paul had in mind when he says that Jesus 'was raised on the third day *in accordance with the Scriptures*' (1 Cor. 15:4). But before we rush ahead, we need to ask what Hosea meant by this verse. Because whether Hosea had in mind the empty tomb is less clear. But he could see that God's people would be destroyed in judgment. He knew that if God were against them, then they would be utterly destroyed. If God tears you apart, then who can heal you?

Yet Hosea believed that somehow God would restore His people. A day would come when God's people would be judged by God. They would be torn apart, destroyed, carried off with no one to rescue them. But God is true to His gracious promises and God is true to His gracious character. And so Hosea believed that somehow God would destroy His people – and then revive them. They would be wiped off the map and wiped out of history. But God would revive them and restore them.

Seven hundred and fifty years or so later, Jesus was arrested and His disciples scattered (Matt. 26:31, 56). There was only one faithful member of the people of God – Jesus. Jesus is not only the Son of God, He is also the people of God. He is our representative. He is the real Israel, the faithful remnant, the true vine.

In the end, there is only one faithful member of the people of God. And on that dark day He was arrested and condemned and crucified. He died and *there was no one left*. God's people were destroyed. God's people were struck down when Jesus our representative was struck down. There were no people of God. It was the end of the line. The story was over. God's purpose was finished. As you look across the whole sweep of human history, there was only one faithful person. The faithful remnant came down to just one person – one true Israelite, one true man of God, one true church member. And now even He is dead. And there was no one left. No one.

But three days later Jesus walked from the tomb. The people who were dead are given new life. The people who were carried away are restored. The story that was over begins a new chapter.

Jesus is our representative. God's people are raised to **live in His presence** when Jesus walked out of the tomb. What Jesus achieved, He achieved on our behalf. If you are a Christian, then when Jesus walked out of the tomb you walked out of the tomb. Or rather *we* walked out of the tomb. It is not just that individuals are promised a future resurrection. The people of God as a collective entity were revived, were brought to new life. When Jesus defeated death, we defeated death. We are in Christ. So His story is our story. His death and resurrection are our death and resurrection. His victory over sin is our victory over sin.

What is Hosea's application of this promise?

> Let us know; let us press on to know the LORD;
> his going out is sure as the dawn;
> he will come to us as the showers,
> as the spring rains that water the earth. (6:3)

Hosea 4:1-3 says: 'There is no faithfulness, no love, no acknowledgment of God in the land ... Because of this the land dries up, and all who live in it waste away.' We are a dry people in a dry land, wasting away because we do not know God. But God will come to revive us and restore us. The picture is of a dry land with no life and no greenery. And then the rains come and it bursts into life again. That is what will happen to God's people.

When God comes, as Hosea promises in verse 2, to revive and restore, then God's people will burst into life. And, says Hosea, God will certainly come – as surely as the sun rises each morning.

Hosea was right. On the third day, God did restore His people. As Jesus walked from the tomb, God's people burst into life. Like a desert blooming as the rains fall, God's people burst into life.

The personal challenge

How can you share the life that Hosea promises and that Jesus achieves through His resurrection? Know God. **Press on to know the LORD.** Do not wait for God to zap you. Press on to know the LORD. Pursue God. Put yourself in a place where you are exposed to His Word. Meet with His people. Read the Bible. Plead with Him. Today you can acknowledge the LORD. Acknowledge Him *as* Lord. Submit your life to Him. Put your faith in Him. And, with Hosea, I promise you: He will come to you – as sure as the dawn. And when He comes, you will burst into life.

The community challenge

But there is also a challenge to us as communities of God's people. Christ rose to create a people, a community, a family. What does that mean? It means we are family. It means our identity is communal. Christians are by definition part of God's people. To become a Christian is to become part of the people for whom Christ died. Romans 12:3-5 says:

> For by the grace given me I say to every one of you: Do not think of yourself more highly than you ought, but rather think of yourself with sober judgment, in accordance with the faith God has distributed to each of you. For just as each of us has one body with many members, and these members do not all have the same function, so in Christ we, though many, form one body, and each member belongs to all the others. (NIV)

Paul says: 'Each member belongs to all the others.' You belong to me and I belong to you. It is strong language! It is the language of ownership and responsibility.

In the New Testament, this communal identity is never abstract or theoretical. It is always expressed in a commitment to a particular community of believers. We do not love the church as an institution or an ideal. We love the brothers and sisters among whom God has placed us. The Christian community is the place where evangelism, pastoral care, discipleship and life all take place.

When you view church as an institution you are likely to talk about church as 'you' or 'they'. You will say things like '*You* need to …' or '*They* don't do this'. But we should see ourselves as part of the people of God revived through the resurrection. Community is an integral part of our identity in Christ. When you see yourself in this way, you will say things like, '*We* need to …' or '*We* could do this.'

This communal identity means taking responsibility for one another and for the life of the community as a whole:

taking the initiative to contribute in prayer times, to wash up, to welcome visitors, to drop in on people, to resolve conflict, to care for needs. Not just *doing* these things, but *taking the initiative to do* these things. If your community does not pray with one another or care for one another or welcome visitors, then do not complain about this. Instead, be the person who initiates prayer, who cares, who welcomes. Be the solution.

Who in the story of the Bible creates community? Is it Abraham and Sarah who are old and barren? Is it the people of Israel who are divided and faithless? Is it the disciples who abandon Jesus in His hour of need? All the way through it is *God* who makes us family – through the death of His Son and the life of His Spirit.

I suspect there are two groups of people reading this chapter. Some people do not take church seriously enough. By that I mean that you do not see it as your *identity*. At best, it is this event that you 'do' from time to time. To you I say: God has made us *family* in Christ. Family is who you are. *So enjoy living in community.* Live out that identity. Get stuck in.

But I suspect there are other people who are worn out trying to create community. Or frustrated that their church is not all they might wish it to be. To you I want to say: *God* has made us family *in Christ*. Community is not something you achieve. It is something Christ achieved through the cross and resurrection. His resurrection revived the people of God, giving us our communal life. It is not something you create. It is something the Holy Spirit creates. *So enjoy living in community.* Do not sit there fretting about its failings. Enjoy what God has done. Enjoy your church.

Dietrich Bonhoeffer, the German pastor and martyr, once wrote these words:

> Those who dream of [an] idealised community demand that it be fulfilled by God, by others, and by themselves. They enter the community of Christians with their demands, set up their own law, and judge one another and even God accordingly … [We] can never live by our own words and deeds, but only by that one Word and deed that really binds us together, the forgiveness of sins in Jesus Christ … Christian community is not an ideal we have to realise, but rather a reality created by God in Christ in which we may participate. The more

clearly we learn to recognise that the ground and strength and promise of all our community is in Jesus Christ alone, the more calmly we will learn to think about our community and pray and hope for it.[2]

Are local churches perfect? Of course not. The thing is, they are not some institution or ideal. They are the people in the room with you. Broken people. Hurting people. Busy people. Struggling people. Do not complain that your community is not meeting your needs – they are just as needy as you. Do not berate them. Love them. Enjoy them.

Churches are amazing. I know sometimes there are problems and tensions. But each one is a miracle. Each one is the cross is action. Each one is the sign of the resurrection. Each one is a direct work of God's Spirit. There is nowhere else where such different people come together, where broken people find a home, where grace is experienced, where God is present by His Spirit. There are plenty of other social groups in our city. But nowhere else where such a diverse people come together as family. It is a beautiful thing. God has made us *family* through the cross and resurrection. So enjoy living in community.

STUDY QUESTIONS

1. What signs of God's coming judgment do we see in history?

2. How might we create hell for ourselves?

3. Which images of God's judgment in Hosea 5 grip your imagination?

4. How can God be both the tearer and healer?

5. What does Hosea have in mind when he says 'on the third day he will raise us up' (6:2)? How is this fulfilled by Jesus?

6. How does Hosea 6:1-3 apply to unbelievers? To believers? To you?

7. How could you 'be the solution' in your church?

---

2.   Dietrich Bonhoeffer, *Life Together* and *Psalms: Prayerbook of the Bible*, Fortress, 2005, 36-8.

Questions for Personal Reflection

1. What does it mean for you to 'press on to the know the LORD' (6:3)?

2. When you talk about your church, do you say 'they', 'you' or 'we'?

3. Some Christians do not take their communal identity seriously enough. Other Christians act as if community is something they must achieve. Where would you position yourself? How does Hosea 6:1-3 speak to you?

6

God Exposes Our Sin
(Hosea 6:4–7:16)

Warning: Hosea 6–7 will not flatter you! In these chapters, God describes Israel's instability and infidelity. He says the nation is like a morning mist (6:4), an overheated oven (7:4), a half-baked loaf (7:8), a deluded old man (7:9), a senseless bird (7:11), a self-preoccupied prayer (7:14) and a faulty bow (7:16).

And Israel is a picture of all humanity. In 6:7, God says: **like Adam they transgressed the covenant; there they dealt faithlessly with me.** Israel are behaving like Adam, the father of the human race. In other words, they are simply being human. They are behaving in a human way. And not human as God created us to be, but human as we are in Adam, with an inbuilt bias towards sin. So we will see ourselves in Hosea's portrait of Israel.

Like a morning mist (6:4-6)
In 6:1-3, Hosea issued an invitation to Israel. He invited them to return to God. Did they respond? It seems any immediate response was short-lived because in verses 4-6 God likens their love to morning mist.

> ⁴What shall I do with you, O Ephraim?
> What shall I do with you, O Judah?
> Your love is like a morning cloud,
> like the dew that goes early away.

[5]Therefore I have hewn them by the prophets;
I have slain them by the words of my mouth,
and my judgment goes forth as the light.
[6]For I desire steadfast love and not sacrifice,
the knowledge of God rather than burnt offerings.

God's questions capture His pain. He longs to embrace them, but they refuse to return with any sincerity. The word **love** in verse 4 is the word used to describe God's covenant love, His steadfast love, His loyalty. God has bound Himself in a covenant or a contract to love us and He sticks to that covenant love. Psalm 136 says that 'his steadfast love endures forever.' And just in case we did not get the message, it repeats this refrain twenty-six times. 'His steadfast love endures forever.'

What about our love? Our love is like morning mist or dew. God's love endures for ever. But our love barely lasts until mid-morning. We know what this is like. I hung the washing out on the line this week, first thing in the morning, and I had to put my boots on because the grass was so wet with drizzle and dew. But by mid-morning I was out in the garden in just my slippers. All the dew had gone. And that was an English spring day. Imagine what that is like in the Middle East.

How long does your love last? Is there a gap between your expressions of love for God on Sunday morning and your life on Monday morning?

These verses take us back to the court summons of 4:1 where 'no steadfast love' was one of the three accusations made against God's people. Here more evidence is being presented before the court. In chapter 4, the focus was on proving the accusation that there is no knowledge or acknowledgment. Now God substantiates His claim that there is no covenant loyalty.

Verse 5 says: **Therefore I have hewn them by the prophets; I have slain them by the words of my mouth, and my judgment goes forth as the light**. When God made a covenant with Israel through Moses, He promised blessings for obedience and curses for disobedience (Deut. 27–28). The prophets reiterated those blessings and curses. God's word is always true. What He proclaims by His word always comes to pass. So His word of curse would be what led to judgment on Israel if she continued in her disobedience. This word spoken by the prophets would hew God's people and slay them.

God acts through His word. When He spoke to the darkness, there was light. His word brings the world into being. And God continues to rule through His word and judge through His word. So the New Testament describes God's word as 'the sword of the Spirit' (Eph. 6:17). 'For the word of God is living and active, sharper than any two-edged sword, piercing to the division of soul and of spirit, of joints and of marrow, and discerning the thoughts and intentions of the heart' (Heb. 4:12). When Jesus rides out in judgment, we read: 'From his mouth comes a sharp sword with which to strike down the nations, and he will rule them with a rod of iron' (Rev. 19:15). When we proclaim the gospel we bring life to some. But that word of Jesus that we speak brings judgment to others (2 Cor. 2:16).

Verse 6 says: **For I desire steadfast love and not sacrifice, the knowledge of God rather than burnt offerings**. It suggests that the people may have made some response to Hosea's invitation in verses 1-3, but it was superficial. They renewed their religious duties, but without any true love or acknowledgement of God. The word **love** in verses 4 and 6 is the same (a fact masked by the NIV's translation of the word as 'mercy' in verse 6). It is the word for 'steadfast love' or 'covenant love'.

God wants our love, not our sacrifices. Think about a human marriage. Which husband wants a wife who serves his meals at six every evening, but does not love him? Who wants a wife who serves with resentment, who serves while she dreams of the lovers she wishes she could have? Who wants a cold, loveless marriage of mere formality and duty? Religious duties without love for God are an attempt to manipulate or bribe Him. God does not want our rituals. He wants our hearts. And when our hearts are not in it, our rituals become a burden to God. Isaiah, Hosea's contemporary, put it like this:

> [11]'What to me is the multitude of your sacrifices?
> says the LORD;
> I have had enough of burnt offerings of rams
> and the fat of well-fed beasts;
> I do not delight in the blood of bulls,
> or of lambs, or of goats.
> [12]When you come to appear before me,
> who has required of you
> this trampling of my courts?

[13]Bring no more vain offerings;
    incense is an abomination to me.
New moon and Sabbath and the calling of convocations –
    I cannot endure iniquity and solemn assembly.
[14]Your new moons and your appointed feasts
    my soul hates;
they have become a burden to me;
    I am weary of bearing them.
[15]When you spread out your hands,
    I will hide my eyes from you;
even though you make many prayers,
    I will not listen;
    your hands are full of blood.
[16]Wash yourselves; make yourselves clean;
    remove the evil of your deeds from before my eyes;
cease to do evil,
    [17]learn to do good;
seek justice,
    correct oppression;
bring justice to the fatherless,
    plead the widow's cause. (Isa.1:11-17)

Or again in Isaiah 58:2-3 God says:

Yet they seek me daily
    and delight to know my ways,
as if they were a nation that did righteousness
    and did not forsake the judgment of their God;
they ask of me righteous judgments;
    they delight to draw near to God.
'Why have we fasted, and you see it not?
    Why have we humbled ourselves, and you take no know-
ledge of it?' Behold, in the day of your fast you seek your own
pleasure,
    and oppress all your workers.

The people seek God on a daily basis. They are assiduous
in their performance of religious duties such as fasting. Yet
really they seek themselves. 'You seek our own pleasure,' says
Isaiah. They seek God only for what they can get from God.
This is why they are quick to complain when God does not
deliver. Moreover, they oppress other people, as the rest of
Isaiah 58 goes on to highlight.

Jesus says the same thing to the religious leaders of his day. He quotes Hosea 6:6 in Matthew 9:10-13 and 12:7.

> And as Jesus reclined at table in the house, behold, many tax collectors and sinners came and were reclining with Jesus and his disciples. And when the Pharisees saw this, they said to his disciples, 'Why does your teacher eat with tax collectors and sinners?' But when he heard it, he said, 'Those who are well have no need of a physician, but those who are sick. Go and learn what this means, "I desire mercy, and not sacrifice." For I came not to call the righteous, but sinners' (Matt. 9:10-13).

In Matthew 12, the religious leaders see the disciples of Jesus picking ears of corn on the Sabbath and accuse them of doing what is unlawful. Jesus cites the Old Testament where the spirit of the law overrides the religious leaders' interpretation of the law. Then he says:

> I tell you, something greater than the temple is here. And if you had known what this means, "I desire mercy, and not sacrifice," you would not have condemned the guiltless. For the Son of Man is lord of the Sabbath (Matt. 12:6-8).

Jesus speaks to us now through the Spirit. 'I don't want you going through the motions. I don't want you just attending meetings. I don't want you serving when it's convenient to you. I want your heart. I want your love. I want a love that puts others first, a love that delights to share your life and your possessions and your time and your emotions with your congregation.'

We cannot simply attend church on Sunday without a commitment to serving others and making Christ known. But the next step is not simply to try harder. The next step is to rediscover a delight in God and His steadfast love. The next steps is 6:3: 'Let us know; let us press on to know the LORD; his going out is sure as the dawn; he will come to us as the showers, as the spring rains that water the earth.'

Like an overheated oven (6:7–7:7)

Hosea 7:5-7 appears to tell the story of an assassination. The princes become drunk and perhaps hatch their plot. Through the night their angry resolve grows. In the morning they strike. **They devour their rulers.** In Hosea's time King Zechariah was assassinated by Shallum. 2 Kings 15:10 says: 'Shallum the son of Jabesh conspired against him and struck him down at Ibleam and put him to death and reigned in his place.' Shallum was himself assassinated within a month by Menahem (2 Kings 15:13-15). Menahem reigned for ten unhappy years before being succeeded by his son, Pekahiah (2 Kings 15:17-22). Pekahiah was then assassinated by Pekah (2 Kings 15:23-26). And finally Pekah was assassinated by Hoshea (2 Kings 15:27-31). Hosea could be referring to any one of these murders (although, as we shall see, there are some indications Hosea could have had Pekahiah's assassination by Pekah in mind). But perhaps the plural **princes, rulers** and **kings** suggests he is describing the *pattern* of assassination in the northern kingdom. The end result is that: **All their kings have fallen.**

It is easy for us to read the history of Israel and feel superior. How could they be so faithless after all God had done for them? But 6:7 says: **But like Adam they transgressed the covenant; there they dealt faithlessly with me.** This is not just a problem with the descendants of Abraham (Israel), but with the descendants of Adam (all humanity). God placed humanity in the garden and Israel in the land. There He promised security and blessing, asking us in return to trust His word. But we turned away. We were unfaithful (5:7; 6:7). We *are* unfaithful.

> [8]Gilead is a city of evildoers,
>   tracked with blood.
> [9]As robbers lie in wait for a man,
>   so the priests band together;
> they murder on the way to Shechem;
>   they commit villainy. (6:8-9)

If people are not faithful to God, then they will not be faithful towards one another. Turning from God leads to a breakdown in social relationships. So violent crime was rife in Israel.

When Pekah assassinated King Pekahiah, he was accompanied by fifty men from **Gilead**: 'And Pekah the son of Remaliah, his captain, conspired against him with fifty men of the people of Gilead, and struck him down in Samaria, in the citadel of the king's house with Argob and Arieh; he put him to death and reigned in his place' (2 Kings 15:25). So this may be why Hosea singles out Gilead as **a city of evildoers**. Hosea does not actually say that bands of robbers are terrorising the highways. Rather, that is the picture he uses to describe the actions of the priests. They act '*as* robbers'. It is not that the priests were indulging in a bit of armed crime on the side. Rather, Hosea is describing their involvement in one of the violent coups.

> ¹⁰In the house of Israel I have seen a horrible thing;
>   Ephraim's whoredom is there; Israel is defiled.
> ¹¹For you also, O Judah, a harvest is appointed.

How does God view their sin? It is **a horrible thing** in His sight. The horrible thing that God sees in Israel may be the violence of verses 8-9. But it is probably the whoredom of the next line. The visible manifestation of this spiritual apostasy was manifold, but perhaps Hosea has in mind the golden calves at Dan and Bethel.

It is not just the northern kingdom that God sees, for here we have another reference to the southern kingdom of Judah. **For you also, O Judah, a harvest is appointed** is ambiguous because in the Bible a harvest can be positive (a harvest of blessing) or negative (a harvest of judgment). The context here, though, suggests it is a harvest of judgment.

> ¹¹When I restore the fortunes of my people.
> ⁷:¹When I would heal Israel,
>   the iniquity of Ephraim is revealed,
>   and the evil deeds of Samaria;
> for they deal falsely;
>   the thief breaks in,
>   and the bandits raid outside.
> ²But they do not consider
>   that I remember all their evil.
> Now their deeds surround them;
>   they are before my face. (6:11–7:2)

In 6:1, Hosea had invited the people to return to God: 'Come, let us return to the LORD; for he has torn us, that he may heal us; he has struck us down, and he will bind us up.' Now

God Himself reiterates His willingness to restore and heal. But these verses again suggest that any responses to Hosea's invitation to repent in 6:1-3 were short-lived. It is almost as if God is willing to come to heal His people. The people appear to respond positively and invite God to come to heal them. So God sets out to heal them. But in fact when He turns up He finds violence instead of repentance. The people think their sins are a light matter that can readily be forgotten because they are of little import. But God remembers (7:2). Our sins are always before him (7:2).

> [3]By their evil they make the king glad,
> and the princes by their treachery.
> [4]They are all adulterers;
> they are like a heated oven
> whose baker ceases to stir the fire,
> from the kneading of the dough until it is leavened.
> [5]On the day of our king, the princes
> became sick with the heat of wine;
> he stretched out his hand with mockers.
> [6]For with hearts like an oven they approach their intrigue;
> all night their anger smoulders;
> in the morning it blazes like a flaming fire.
> [7]All of them are hot as an oven,
> and they devour their rulers.
> All their kings have fallen,
> and none of them calls upon me.

Instead of condemning evil, the political leaders delight in it (7:3) and participate in it (7:5). There is a real sense of complicity in these verses. The priests are involved in banditry (6:9) while the kings celebrate in evil (7:3). Even when they get into trouble, they do not call on God (7:7).

This is a reminder of the importance of praying for our political leaders as Paul urges us in 1 Timothy 2:1-2: 'First of all, then, I urge that supplications, prayers, intercessions, and thanksgivings be made for all people, for kings and all who are in high positions, that we may lead a peaceful and quiet life, godly and dignified in every way.'

Both God's people and their kings are like an overheated oven. Their passion for evil smoulders (7:6), without needing stoking (7:4). They are, as it were, on fire for sin. As a result, they are consumed by their own sin (7:7). Sin feeds sin. Giving in to temptation fuels further temptation as we experience the (temporary) pleasures of sin. The fire of sin burns stronger in our hearts until it begins to consume us.

Can you detect patterns of sin in your life? Can you see ways in which succumbing to temptation has fuelled further temptation? Turn to God in repentance. He says: **'I would restore the fortunes of my people ... I would heal Israel'** (6:11–7:1).

The focus of Hosea 6:6–7:7 was Israel's internal politics and plotting. The focus of Hosea 7:8-16 is her foreign policy. In chapters 4–5, Hosea spoke of her spiritual infidelity. Here he speaks of her political infidelity.

God had promised to protect and provide for His people. From the exodus onwards, He had an amazing track record of delivering them against the odds (7:15). But now Ephraim (another name for Israel) **mixes with the nations** (7:8). The people turn to Egypt and then to Assyria for help (7:11) instead of turning to God, even though He **longs to redeem them** (7:13).

In 7:8-16, the images Hosea uses in his anatomy of human infidelity come thick and fast.

Like a half-baked loaf (7:8)

> Ephraim mixes himself with the peoples;
>> Ephraim is a cake not turned.

A cake that is **not turned** over will be burnt on one side and remain uncooked on the other. It is neither one thing nor the other. In the same way, Israel is not a pagan nation, but neither is it a holy nation. It is like the church at Laodicea to whom the risen Christ says: 'I know your works: you are neither cold nor hot. Would that you were either cold or hot! So, because you are lukewarm, and neither hot nor cold, I will spit you out of my mouth.' (Rev. 3:15-16)

Ephraim mixes himself with the peoples and so is unfit for purpose – the purpose of displaying God's goodness to the nations. God has set apart Israel as a holy nation. They were to be distinct from the nations so that through their distinctiveness they could display God's character among the nations. They were to be holy as God is holy. But if Israel mixes with the nations then it can no longer perform this role. Its central purpose as a nation is lost. The more Israel becomes like the nations, the less it has to offer.

It is the same today for the church. It is tempting to think that we should become like the world to reach the world. Clearly there is an appropriate adaptation to our context. Paul says: 'I have become all things to all people, that by all means I might save some' (1 Cor. 9:22). We should avoid unnecessary barriers to the gospel. But the more we become like the world around us, the less we have to offer. It is our distinctiveness that will attract people – even if it also repels some. The hope of the world is the gospel of Jesus. We adapt so that the gospel can be seen and heard. But we refuse to compromise, so that it is the gospel that is heard and not some poor echo of the culture. Paul continues: 'I do it all for the sake of the gospel, that I may share with them in its blessings' (1 Cor. 9:23). What drives him is the gospel – not a desire to be trendy or fit in.

Like a deluded old man (7:9-10)

> 9Strangers devour his strength,
>   and he knows it not;
> grey hairs are sprinkled upon him,
>   and he knows it not.
> 10The pride of Israel testifies to his face;
>   yet they do not return to the LORD their God,
>   nor seek him, for all this.

We are to imagine an obviously ageing man who still acts like a teenager. My daughters often exclaim at how out of touch with current trends I am. But I point out that there is something worse than an unfashionable middle-aged man and that is a middle-aged man trying to be fashionable! Israel is like a man who cannot grow old gracefully. Or like an old man who still attempts the exploits of his youth that he can now no longer achieve. Back in the days of David and Solomon, Israel was a major power. But now it has lost its power and is overreaching itself. Hosea was ministering at a time when Israel had known a long period of prosperity. Those days would soon be over, but she will not recognise it. More importantly, she will not return to the LORD – the source of her former power and prestige.

Like a senseless bird (7:11-13)

[11]Ephraim is like a dove,
  silly and without sense,
  calling to Egypt, going to Assyria.
[12]As they go, I will spread over them my net;
  I will bring them down like birds of the heavens;
  I will discipline them according to the report made to their
congregation.
[13]Woe to them, for they have strayed from me!
  Destruction to them, for they have rebelled against me!
I would redeem them,
  but they speak lies against me.

Israel is like a silly dove, flitting about, never settling, never committing. Sometimes Israel tried to form an alliance with Egypt; sometimes it bought off Assyria with tribute. All the time she ignored her fundamental problem: her spiritual adultery. So God will catch them in His net of judgment. **As they go** has the sense of 'whichever way they go'. In other words, it does not matter whether they go to Egypt or Assyria. Either way they will end up in the net of God's judgment.

It is not difficult to feel the relevance of this image today. Idolatrous desires or their insecurities can so control people that they flit about from one thing to another, seeking fulfilment. It might be someone pursuing the latest trends. It might be someone jumping from one lover to another. It might be someone switching their money from one investment to another. We seek fulfilment and security in things other than God and do not find them. So we move from one thing to another like a senseless dove. 'Those who cling to worthless idols forfeit the grace that could be theirs' (Jonah 2:8, NIV). We never arrive at a place of rest because we never seek rest in the right place. As Augustine famously prayed, 'Our hearts are restless until they find their rest in you.'

Again we get a glimpse of God's heartbreak over His people. **I would redeem them, but they speak lies against me** (7:13).

Like a self-preoccupied prayer (7:14)

They do not cry to me from the heart,
  but they wail upon their beds;

for grain and wine they gash themselves;
they rebel against me.

They do not cry to me from the heart, says God. But that does not mean they have stopped praying. When the people pray or gather for worship they are not really turning to God. Instead, their cry is just a self-pitying wail in which they bemoan their lot. They cry out, but they do not cry to God. Or rather they do not cry out from the heart. They cry out to God, but they are not really interested in God. It is not for God they cry. Instead, they are only interested in the wine He might give. It was the same in Jesus' day. The crowds in John 6 come after Jesus because they want Him to provide bread. But He Himself is the bread – the Bread of Life. God gives us many blessings in the gospel. But at the heart of the gospel is God Himself. What we get is God Himself. And if our interest is just in God's stuff, as it were, then God will wean us from our misplaced affections. He wants our undivided loyalty. He is worthy of our undivided affection.

The people's prayer life is frequent and fervent. **They wail upon their beds** and **gash themselves**. But frequent and fervent prayer is not necessarily a sign of spiritual health. Indeed, it is usually a sign of faithlessness. Jesus said: 'when you pray, do not heap up empty phrases as the Gentiles do, for they think that they will be heard for their many words. Do not be like them, for your Father knows what you need before you ask him' (Matt. 6:7-8). Pagan people think they can manipulate God and they think they need to manipulate Him. They pray as if they need to wear God down until He finally concedes to their request. But the true child of God can present her requests to God and leave them there. She will not try to manipulate Him because she does not need to, and knows she cannot. Instead, she relates to God as her loving heavenly Father.

Like a faulty bow (7:15-16)

[15]Although I trained and strengthened their arms,
yet they devise evil against me.
[16]They return, but not upward;
they are like a treacherous bow;

their princes shall fall by the sword
　　because of the insolence of their tongue.
This shall be their derision in the land of Egypt.

God had always protected His people when they turned to Him for help, equipping them for battle. They are trained by God, but they use their skill against Him (7:15). They return, but they do not return upwards to God (7:16). They are like a faulty bow. They are like a fairground rifle. You point it at the target, but the bullet always veers off course. They make a show of repentance, but they do not redirect their lives to God. Like a faulty bow, full of energy, they fire off towards God. But then they bend away from Him and miss the target.

That is what humanity is like. You point us in God's direction. You say, 'This is your God, your help, your protection, your joy, your security, your salvation.' We head off towards Him. But soon we are veering off in a different direction.

That is what I am like. That is what it feels like when I meet with my Christian community. I am pointed again in the right direction. There in front of me is my God, my true hope, joy, security and satisfaction. But then when I am on my own I veer off in another direction. I look for joy and affirmation elsewhere. So I need people who are sharing their lives with me, speaking of Jesus day by day. This is why the New Testament says: 'Encourage one another *daily*, as long as it is called Today, so that none of you may be hardened by sin's deceitfulness' (Heb. 3:13). This is why we need to encourage one another with the love of God. We need to speak of God's love to us in Christ so that our love remains constant. Only as we love God will we *want* to share our lives, give generously, have people in our homes, do mission together. Hebrews 10:24 says: 'Let us consider how to stir up one another to love and good works.'

STUDY QUESTIONS

1. Hosea 6–7 says that people are like a morning mist (6:4), an overheated oven (7:4), a half-baked loaf (7:8), a deluded old man (7:9), a senseless bird (7:11), a self-preoccupied prayer (7:14) and a faulty bow (7:16). Which of these images of human sin grip your imagination?

2. How does God view our sin?

3. Hosea and Jesus say: 'I desire mercy, and not sacrifice' (Hosea 6:6; Matt. 9:10-13; 12:7). What might this look like for you?

4. Identify examples of appropriate cultural adaptation.

5. Identify examples of inappropriate cultural compromise.

6. What makes the difference between these appropriate and inappropriate attempts at cultural adaptation?

7. Identity examples of a restlessness that comes from pursuing fulfilment apart from God.

Questions for Personal Reflection

1. Hosea 7:14 says: 'They do not cry to me from the heart, but they wail upon their beds; for grain and wine they gash themselves; they rebel against me.' In what ways might your prayers be self-pitying or self-indulgent or an attempt to manipulate God?

2. In what ways does the message of Matthew 6:5-15 protect us from these dangers when we pray?

3. Hebrews 3:13 suggests that we need daily encouragement to follow God in the face of the deceitfulness of sin described in Hosea 6–7. How might you find this? How might you provide this for other people?

7

God Unmasks Our Delusions
(Hosea 8:1-14)

In 5:8, Hosea called for the trumpet to be sounded as a warning of God's coming judgment. In chapter 8, God calls for that trumpet warning to be sounded again:

> Set the trumpet to your lips!
> One like a vulture is over the house of the LORD,
> because they have transgressed my covenant
>   and rebelled against my law. (8:1)

The word **vulture** could be 'eagle'. The NIV reads: **An eagle is over the house of the LORD.** An eagle is hovering over Israel in the form of the Assyrian army. It is appropriate for an Assyrian threat to be represented as an eagle as eagles often appear in Assyrian art as guardian deities. But the repeated use of **my** in the second half of verse 1 makes it clear that this will be God's doing. The eagle of Assyrian invasion hovers over Israel, ready at any movement to swoop down and attack with terrifying speed and power. The reason is that the people have broken God's covenant. But the problem is that they cannot see this because they are deluded.

1. People think they know God, but they do not (8:2-3)

> ²To me they cry,
>   My God, we – Israel – know you.
> ³Israel has spurned the good;
>   the enemy shall pursue him.

Chapter 4 opened with God's court case against Israel. God's accusation was that 'there is ... no acknowledgment of God in the land' (4:1; 5:4). But now the people repudiate this charge. **We – Israel – know you**, they cry.

But God rejects this claim. In Deuteronomy 30:15, God gave Israel a choice between 'life and good, death and evil' and they chose to reject what is good (8:3). The word **spurn** (zanah) in verse 3 echoes the word 'whoredom' (zana) in 1:2, where Hosea is told to 'take to yourself a wife of whoredom and have children of whoredom, for the land commits great whoredom by forsaking the LORD.' The people have, as it were, whored away from what is good. People can say the right things, but not know God. And they can do the right things, but not be faithful to Him if their behaviour is an attempt to save themselves.

At the end of the Sermon on the Mount, Jesus says, 'Not everyone who says to me, "Lord, Lord", will enter the kingdom of heaven, but only he who does the will of my Father who is in heaven' (Matt. 7:21). There will be many who prophesied in His name or performed miracles to whom He says, 'I never knew you. Away from me, you evildoers!' (7:23) They assume they know God, but God does not know them. It is a salutary and sobering statement. How are we to respond? Can we have assurance as Christians? Can we have confidence in our salvation? Jesus goes on to tell the parable of the houses of the rock and sand:

> Therefore everyone who hears these words of mine and puts them into practice is like a wise man who built his house on the rock. The rain came down, the streams rose, and the winds blew and beat against that house; yet it did not fall, because it had its foundation on the rock. But everyone who hears these words of mine and does not put them into practice is like a foolish man who built his house on sand. The rain came down, the streams rose, and the winds blew and beat against that house, and it fell with a great crash (Matt. 7:24-27).

We can have confidence if we build our lives on the rock of Jesus' words. There is assurance in the gospel. If we are trusting in the finished work of Christ, then we can have complete confidence because He will prove a sure foundation. But if we are trusting in our works, then we cannot have confidence, even if they are miraculous works. This is the delusion of religious people. 'I knew you,' they say. 'I served you.' But in truth they were serving themselves. And what they were trusting was themselves. So Jesus will say to them, 'I never knew you.'

2. People think they rule under God, but they do not (8:4)

> They made kings, but not through me.
> They set up princes, but I knew it not.

This is an allusion both to the beginning and end of Israel's history. In 1 Samuel 8, the people of Israel ask for a king. God had said Israel would be ruled by a king under him (Deut. 17). But their request was a rejection of God as King. They wanted to be ruled like other nations. They wanted to rule themselves. **They made kings, but not through me.** The final years of the northern kingdom of Israel were marked by a series of bloody coups (2 Kings 15). The people were setting up their own kings. But more fundamentally they had rejected God as their King.

3. People think they worship God, but they do not (8:4-6)

> ⁴With their silver and gold they made idols
>   for their own destruction.
> ⁵I have spurned your calf, O Samaria.
>   My anger burns against them.
> How long will they be incapable of innocence?
> ⁶For it is from Israel;
> a craftsman made it;
>   it is not God.
> The calf of Samaria
>   shall be broken to pieces.

The people's lives were full of worship. No doubt they thought of themselves as religious people. But it was false worship.

While Moses was on Mount Sinai receiving the covenant from God, down below the people were restless and doubting. They persuaded Aaron, the brother of Moses, to 'make us gods who shall go before us' (Exod. 32:1). So Aaron collected their gold jewellery. 'And he received the gold from their hand and fashioned it with a graving tool and made a golden calf. And they said, "These are your gods, O Israel, who brought you up out of the land of Egypt!"' (Exod. 32:4). The golden calf was, in a sense, Israel's original sin and it set the pattern for the rest of their history. The sin of Israel during the exodus was constantly revisited.

Years later, King Solomon had put a man called Jeroboam in charge of his forced labour. But Jeroboam had to escape into exile in Egypt after he 'lifted up his hand against the king' (1 Kings 11:26-40). When Rehoboam became king after the death of Solomon, he increased the forced labour of the people even more than his father had done. So Jeroboam returned to lead the rebellion that created the northern kingdom of Israel. The people were enduring the slavery of forced labour just as they had done in Egypt. Now a man had come from Egypt to lead the people from slavery to freedom (1 Kings 12:1-4). So it looked for a brief period like Jeroboam might be a new Moses. But his first act was to set up the two golden calves at Bethel and Dan (1 Kings 12:25-33). Rather than being a new Moses, Jeroboam turned out to be a new Aaron.

But by the time of Hosea the calf in Dan was no longer under Israelite control. That is why he refers to just one calf. So **the calf of Samaria** in verse 6 is not a description of its location, but of its owner. In verse 5, it is **your calf**, that is the calf that belongs to Samaria. Samaria was the capital city of Israel and is often used in the Old Testament to represent the nation as a whole. The people used their silver and gold to make idols. But Hosea has already told us that it was God who gave it to them: 'And she did not know that it was I … who lavished on her silver and gold, which they used for Baal' (2:8). They used the wealth God gave them to make idols to replace Him.

The word **spurned** in verse 5 (**I have spurned your calf**) echoes verse 3 (**Israel has spurned the good**) (the NIV translates this word as 'reject' in verse 3 and 'throw out' in verse 5). The meaning of verse 5 is unclear. It could mean God will reject Israel for rejecting Him (ESV), in which case the punishment matches the crime. Or it could mean Israel should reject their idolatry instead of rejecting God (NIV), in which case the repentance matches the crime.

Their idols are **from Israel** and made by **a metalworker**. In other words, they are not God! Hosea is echoing the unmasking of idolatry by Isaiah, his contemporary. Isaiah 44:9 says: 'All who fashion idols are nothing, and the things they delight in do not profit.' Isaiah describes in detail the process by which an idol is made. His point is simple. People think idols can save them or provide for them. But the reality is that idols are wholly dependent on human beings. He describes how the wood used for making an idol is also used to cook a meal. In other words, the idol is no different from ordinary cooking fuel: 'Half of it he burns in the fire. Over the half he eats meat; he roasts it and is satisfied. Also he warms himself and says, "Aha, I am warm, I have seen the fire!" And the rest of it he makes into a god, his idol, and falls down to it and worships it. He prays to it and says, "Deliver me, for you are my god!"' (Isa. 44:16-17). (See also Isa. 2:8, 20; 40:18-20; Jer. 10:1-16.)

4. People think human help can save, but it does not (8:7-10)
A common delusion of people is to think actions have no consequences, certainly no consequences in relation to God. Peter describes this attitude in 2 Peter 3:3-4: 'Scoffers will come in the last days with scoffing, following their own sinful desires. They will say, "Where is the promise of his coming? For ever since the fathers fell asleep, all things are continuing as they were from the beginning of creation."' Hosea addresses this delusion with a proverb:

For they sow the wind,
  and they shall reap the whirlwind. (8:7)

Sowing in a wind could be positive, with the wind distributing the seed. But here it should be understood in a negative way, with the wind taking the seed away from its intended target. Elsewhere, the wind is used to describe pointless work whose rewards are elusive. 'I have seen everything that is done under the sun, and behold, all is vanity and a striving after wind' (Eccles. 1:14). 'This also is a grievous evil: just as he came, so shall he go, and what gain is there to him who toils for the wind?' (Eccles. 5:16). Hosea himself says: 'Ephraim feeds on the wind and pursues the east wind all day long; they multiply falsehood and violence' (12:1).

This proverb forces the reader to pause. It describes situations in which there is an inevitable link between a given cause and a certain effect. In other words, if you do a certain action you can be sure that certain consequences will follow. If you pull a cat's tail it will turn on you. 'Whoever troubles his own household will inherit the wind' (Prov. 11:29).

But the twist with this proverb is that it describes situations in which the consequences are larger than the actions that precipitated them. A small action leads to a much larger consequence. We can all think of situations in which this happens in life. We lie to avoid embarrassment. But then, to maintain the pretence, we are forced into larger and larger lies. Eventually, we are found out and the consequences far exceed the initial embarrassment we hoped to avoid. We sow a 'small' lie and reap widespread exposure. Or a second glance leads to a sexual fantasy that leads to a liaison that then must be covered up. We sow a second glance and reap a wrecked marriage. This is what happened to King David in 2 Samuel 11–12 and he reaped murder, death and civil war.

The delusion of irreligious people is 'I'm OK because my actions have no consequences. It doesn't hurt anyone.' But actions, says Hosea, do have consequences. And those consequences may be far more significant than we ever dreamed. Israel's actions will come back to bite them. The very things they pursue will be turned against them.

Verse 7 sets out this principle. The practice for Israel was that their hope was misplaced. They thought an alliance with Assyria would save them. But not only would it not save them, it would actually make matters worse. They would sow the wind and reap the whirlwind.

The reference to sowing and reaping is not incidental. Baal worship was a fertility cult that promised good harvests. Hosea agrees. Sowing to the Baals will indeed reap a harvest. But it is a harvest of divine judgment. The harvest Israel will reap will be a whirlwind of destruction.

> [7]The standing grain has no heads;
>   it shall yield no flour;
> if it were to yield,
>   strangers would devour it.

⁸Israel is swallowed up;
  already they are among the nations
  as a useless vessel.
⁹For they have gone up to Assyria,
  a wild donkey wandering alone;
  Ephraim has hired lovers.
¹⁰Though they hire allies among the nations,
  I will soon gather them up.
And the king and princes shall soon writhe
  because of the tribute.

The harvest Israel will reap is no harvest. In Hebrew, the words **no heads** and **no flour** in verse 7 rhyme. 'The grain has no head, the field yields no bread,' we might say. It makes this a forceful expression of scarcity. Baal was supposed to make the land plentiful, but Baal is powerless in the face of God's judgment. Any literal harvest they receive will be consumed by foreigners. In fact, in verse 8 Israel herself becomes the meal – though not a pleasant one: **Israel is swallowed up; now she is among the nations like something no one wants** (8:8, NIV).

The Hebrew words **donkey** and **Ephraim** have the same consonants. Hebrew is usually written using just the consonants, so in Hebrew these shared consonants tie the words together. It is a pun. Their similar names point to another similarity between Israel and a wild donkey: they are both restless in their search of a partner. Israel should have remained faithful to the LORD and trusted Him for security. But instead she has pursued alliances with other nations. The **hired lovers** is probably a reference to the tribute she paid to secure these alliances. 2 Kings 15:19, for example, says: 'Pul the king of Assyria came against the land, and Menahem gave Pul a thousand talents of silver, that he might help him to confirm his hold on the royal power.' This happened during Hosea's ministry. But it is futile, says Hosea. Instead of buying peace, this offer of tribute has encouraged other nations to come back for more. Often in the Old Testament prophets, God **gathering** His people has a positive connotation of God restoring Israel after they have been scattered by exile. But in verse 10 God speaks of gathering for a harvest of judgment. (See 9:6; Ps. 50:5-7; Ezek. 22:20; Joel 3:2; Micah 4:12; Zeph. 3:8.)

Israel went to Assyria for help. But the solution would become an even bigger problem when the Assyrians came back to destroy them. 'Sow to the wind and reap the whirlwind.'

Christians readily acknowledge that we rely on God. We affirm that He is the source of blessing and success. But in practice we often default to assuming it is our efforts or our skills that will lead to success. There is no better measure of an individual's reliance on God than their commitment to pray. And there is no better measure of a church's reliance on God than the health of its prayer meetings. It is not simply a case of measuring how long we pray. Long prayers often betray a false faith in prayer itself (as if we could manipulate God through long prayers) rather than a faith in a heavenly Father (Matt. 6:7-8). But we should pray as if God's actions matter. A half-hearted commitment to prayer is a sign that we think our role matters more than God's role. We have become self-reliant or reliant on human help.

5. People think religion saves, but it does not (8:11-14)

> [11]Because Ephraim has multiplied altars for sinning,
>   they have become to him altars for sinning.
> [12]Were I to write for him my laws by the ten thousands,
>   they would be regarded as a strange thing.
> [13]As for my sacrificial offerings,
>   they sacrifice meat and eat it,
>   but the LORD does not accept them.
> Now he will remember their iniquity
>   and punish their sins;
>   they shall return to Egypt.
> [14]For Israel has forgotten his Maker
>   and built palaces,
> and Judah has multiplied fortified cities;
>   so I will send a fire upon his cities,
>   and it shall devour her strongholds.

Notice the repeated use of the word **multiplied**. Israel is *full* of religious activity. But it is meaningless. Their self-righteousness is a mask for sin. They have forgotten their Maker (8:14), the God who had made them who they were as a nation (Deut. 32:6). So, just as they **eat** their sacrifices in verse 13, God will **devour** them in verse 14 (it is the same word in Hebrew). He will send fire (*salah*) on their **cities** (*sakah*). Their altars will corrupt them and their allies will turn on them.

God's law was clear. **I wrote for them the many things of my law, but they regarded them as something foreign** (8:12, NIV). There was no room for confusion. But Israel regards it as something foreign. To those who love God, His law is a delight, bringing freedom and joy. But to those who do not love God, His law feels odd, restrictive and arbitrary. We see this today with biblical sexual ethics, and complementarian views of the roles of men and women.

Perhaps Hosea has one law in particular in mind. In Deuteronomy 12, God says that when Israel is settled in the land the LORD will choose one place of worship. The Israelites were only to offer sacrifices at this central location. The aim was probably to ensure worship was free from syncretism. The people were to worship in a way that reflected the character of God and His promises. Ultimately, the worship of the temple was a picture of Christ and His coming salvation. Any deviation from this would muddy the object of true faith. But Israel has not kept this commandment. Instead, they have **multiplied altars for sinning** (8:11).

In verse 13, God remembers, while in verse 14 Israel forgets. Israel has forgotten his Maker. Hosea may have in mind God as the Creator of all things. But he is probably referring to God as the One who created Israel as a nation, who took her from slavery and gave her a land. Hosea's thought here echoes Deuteronomy 32:6: 'Do you thus repay the LORD, you foolish and senseless people? Is not he your father, who created you, who made you and established you?' Israel is who she is because of God. But she has forgotten her history.

The big irony here is found when we contrast verse 14 with verses 5-6. Verses 5-6 says: **'I have spurned your calf ... For it is from Israel; a craftsman made it; it is not God.'** Verse 14 says: **'Israel has forgotten his Maker.'** God is the Maker of Israel. But Israel wants to be the maker of god as she fashions idols.

This delusion that religion saves is as common today as it was in Hosea's day. Religious people still think that they can win God's approval through their religious performance or moral rectitude or outward respectability. They may admit they do wrong things, but they believe that their religious duties will outweigh their wrongdoing in the sight of God. But it is a delusion. Their religion is actually a thing of their own making – just as much as it was for Hosea's **craftsman** (8:6). People compose their rituals and perform their duties. Then they think their god will save them. But the reality is they are relying on themselves and their own actions. We may not have a calf-shaped idol. But we do have things we rely on to bring us satisfaction or to give us meaning or to secure our futures.

This is the attitude exemplified by the Pharisee in the parable Jesus told in Luke 18:9-14. The Pharisee prays: 'God, I thank you that I am not like other men, extortioners, unjust, adulterers, or even like this tax collector. I fast twice a week; I give tithes of all that I get' (Luke 18:11-12). God hardly gets a look-in. He is just mentioned in the opening address. After that, there are two foci to the prayer. First, people who are not as good as the Pharisee ('I thank you that I am not like other men, extortioners, unjust, adulterers, or even like this tax collector'). Pharisees need sinners! They need sinners so they can feel good about themselves. Second, the Pharisee's prayer is full of himself and his good works ('I fast twice a week; I give tithes of all that I get.'). Luke tells us that Jesus 'told this parable to some who trusted in themselves that they were righteous, and treated others with contempt' (Luke 18:9). That is precisely what we see in the Pharisee – trust in his own righteousness and contempt for others. But the punchline of the story is that this Pharisee was not justified in God's sight. It was the repentant sinner who was justified.

There is a secular version of this delusion. People think of themselves as essentially good people. They blame their wrongdoing on their circumstances or hormones or up-bringing. Meanwhile, they claim the credit for their good works for themselves. Like the Pharisees, they need failing people so they can feel good about themselves. If they are of a right-wing bent, they may castigate 'delinquents' for their irresponsibility. If they are of a left-wing bent, they may patronise needy people whom they try to rescue in some way. But in both cases they think of themselves as superior – either to those in need or to those whose uncaring attitudes they despise.

Hosea 8:11 says: **Because Ephraim has multiplied altars for sinning, they have become to him altars for sinning**. Twice Hosea refers to **altars for sinning**. It alludes to the original purpose of altars in Israel. God instituted the systems of altars and sacrifices 'for sin'. That is, sacrifices were given to deal with the problem of sin by atoning for the guilt of sin. The animal died in the place of the worshipper. The sin of the worshipper was symbolically placed on the animal and the animal suffered the consequence of that sin, which is death. It was a pointer to the ultimate sacrifice, of Jesus 'the Lamb of God, who takes away the sin of the world' (John 1:29). The whole sacrifice system is an aid to faith in Jesus, the coming Lamb of God.

But now Hosea is punning on this meaning. Now Israel's altars are 'for sin' in a terrible parody of the original meaning of that phrase. Now they have been occasions not for the forgiveness of sin, but for the committing of sin. The act of offering a sacrifice has become a sinful act. The heart of Israelite faith has become the location of its transgression.

How can this be? Hebrews 11:6 says: 'without faith it is impossible to please him, for whoever would draw near to God must believe that he exists and that he rewards those who seek him.' Hebrews draws the contrast between Abel's sacrifice and Cain's sacrifice. Cain offered a sacrifice, but it brought condemnation because it was not accompanied by faith (Heb. 11:4). The same is true for Israel in Hosea's day, as verse 13 makes clear: **As for my sacrificial offerings, they sacrifice meat and eat it, but the LORD does not accept them**. What saves is not the sacrifice itself, but faith in the reality to which it points. Anything else is an attempt to manipulate God, to buy Him off rather than trust His grace.

This is an important point to realise. Our religious duties can be sinful acts. Attending church, listening to good sermons, praying every day, serving the needy can all be sinful acts if we do them to win God's approval or earn His blessing. They are sinful because they are a denial of His grace. We act as if the cross is not enough and we need to top it up with our own efforts. Or they are sinful because they are an attempt to manipulate God. We assume God is a mean and begrudging father who needs to be cajoled into doing what we want through repeated religious activity or won over through our good deeds.

Consider the man who complains that God has not given him a wife despite his hard work in God's service. Why is this man serving God? Not because he loves God and enjoys His grace. No, he is simply trying to use God to further his own ends – in this case, getting a wife. Outwardly, his behaviour looks righteous and impressive. But in reality his Christian service is 'for sinning'.

The gospel of God's grace unmasks this delusion and undermines its foundation. None of us can feel superior. We are all sinners before the holy God. We are not OK. Our good works do not outweigh our wrongdoing. We are weighed in the scales and found wanting. But in His grace God has sent His Son. His righteousness – or His rightness – is credited to us. And our wrongdoing is credited to Him as He hangs on the cross in our place. In the gospel, we see ourselves as we really are. We are naked and exposed (Heb. 4:12-13). But in that moment of exposure we are clothed with the righteousness of Christ. We are secure in Him. And we now regard others from the perspective of grace. We cannot feel superior. We can only feel grateful for God's grace.

STUDY QUESTIONS

1. Hosea 8 shows that:

   • People think they know God, but they do not (8:2-3).

   • People think they rule under God, but they do not (8:4).

   • People think they worship God, but they do not (8:4-6).

   • People think human help can save, but it does not (8:7-10).

   • People think religion saves, but it does not (8:11-14).

2. Identify examples from your own experience of each of these delusions.

3. With so much potential for delusion, how can we be confident in our salvation?

4. Hosea 8:7 says: 'They sow the wind, and they shall reap the whirlwind.' This will ultimately be fulfilled at the final judgment. But can you identify examples of this principle from your own experience?

5. How would you respond to someone who justified their sinful behaviour by saying, 'It doesn't hurt anyone'?

Questions for Personal Reflection

1. 'Pharisees need sinners.' Are there people you look down on so that you can feel good about yourself? How does the gospel address this attitude?

2. Are you seeking God for God's sake or for the sake of what He might give you?

8

God Reverses Our Story
(Hosea 9:1-17)

I wonder what images and ideas the word 'home' evokes for you? For most people, home represents a place of belonging, a place of security, a place of rest, a place of love. Home is where you can kick off your shoes and not feel you have to impress or win approval.

When God first made humanity, He placed us in a home. Genesis 1:31 says: 'God saw everything that he had made, and behold, it was very good.' The whole world was good. Yet God still plants a garden for humanity. God still makes a specific place that will be home for humanity. The whole world is good, but only Eden is home!

But humanity rebelled against God's rule. God had provided a home for us, a place of plenty and provision, security and safety. But we believed Satan's lie that we would be more free without God. We still believe it every time we sin. We think we will be more free without God, but we end up enslaved by sin and self.

So God judged humanity, and that judgment involved exile. They were exiled from the home God had placed them in. Angels with a flaming sword are placed at the entrance to Eden to prevent them returning. In Genesis 3:24, we are told that God 'drove out the man, and at the east of the garden of Eden he placed the cherubim and a flaming sword that turned every way to guard the way to the tree of life.' Humanity is now east of Eden, away from home, homeless.

When Cain kills his brother Abel, God's judgment is this: 'You will be a restless wanderer on the earth' (Gen. 4:12). His judgment is to be homeless and rootless. 'So Cain went out from the LORD's presence and lived in the land of Nod, east of Eden' (Gen. 4:16). Adam and Eve were east of Eden, away from home. Now Cain is further east, further from home.

But God in His grace comes to Abraham and promises a new beginning. And at the heart of that promise is the promise of a home. God promises Abraham: 'To your offspring I will give this land' (Gen. 12:7).

By the time we get to the book of Exodus, Abraham's family has become a great nation, just as God promised. But they are slaves in Egypt. They are still far from home. They are far from home *geographically* for they are not in the land God had promised to Abraham. And they are far from home *metaphorically* for they are not enjoying the belonging, security and provision that home represents.

But God has not abandoned His promises. He is about to lead them home through what we call the 'exodus'. Under the leadership of Moses, God liberated His people from slavery through the ten plagues, through the Passover, through the parting of the Red Sea. He led His people out to Mount Sinai in the wilderness.

Hosea 9:10 says, **Like grapes in the wilderness, I found Israel. Like the first fruit on the fig tree in its first season, I saw your fathers**. Hosea is alluding to the way God met with Israel in the desert. It was at Mount Sinai that Israel became a nation.

A generation later, Joshua led the people into the Promised Land. God fought for His people and they took the land, driving out most of its inhabitants. God gave them rest in the land, a land flowing with milk and honey. They were home. And home was a place of rest, provision and protection.

This home for Israel was a picture and a pointer to God's ultimate plan: a new home for a new humanity. The book of 2 Peter 3:1 says: 'In keeping with his promise we are looking forward to a new heaven and a new earth, the home of righteousness' (NIV). Our exile from God's presence will be over. Our restless wandering will be over. We will have come home.

Hosea 8:1 said: 'An eagle is over the house of the LORD' (NIV). It is an allusion to Deuteronomy 28:49: 'The LORD will bring a nation against you from far away, from the ends of the earth, like an eagle swooping down.' Now that eagle is hovering over Israel in the form of the Assyrian army. This allusion to Deuteronomy 28 is important because it is taken from the covenant curses that Moses proclaimed to God's people as they were about to enter their new home. In Deuteronomy 27–28, Moses proclaimed the blessings that would flow if the people kept the covenant and the curses that would fall if they disobeyed the covenant. At the heart of those curses was the curse of exile. Israel would be scattered and exiled. She would have no resting place, no home. She would return to Egypt and return to slavery. The exodus would go into reverse.

Now an eagle is hovering over Israel. It seems the implementation of those curses may be imminent. And this is precisely how chapter 8 ends: 'Now he will remember their iniquity and punish their sins; they shall return to Egypt' (8:13). The Bible story goes into reverse, for Israel will return to slavery like the slavery of Egypt. The exodus will be undone. It is a theme to which Hosea returns in chapter 9.

The exodus reversed

> Rejoice not, O Israel!
>   Exult not like the peoples;
> for you have played the whore, forsaking your God.
>   You have loved a prostitute's wages on all threshing floors. (9:1)

In this verse, Hosea is probably speaking to the people during a harvest festival. In 1 Kings 12:32, King Jeroboam instituted festivities to mirror those in Jerusalem (Lev. 23:40; Deut. 16:14-15). In Israelite agriculture, the wheat was beaten to detach the grains from the outer husk (the chaff). The wheat and chaff were separated through being tossed in the air. The wind would blow away the lighter chaff, leaving the wheat behind. So threshing places were normally a communal space in an elevated position where they would catch the wind. This made them ideally suited for local festivities. It may be that Baal worship was now involved, since Baal was a fertility cult. So the reference to prostitution is probably not literal prostitution (or at least not primarily), but to spiritual infidelity.

Perhaps there is a lull in Assyrian aggression and everything looks rosy. But the real problem has not gone away for the real problem is the problem of God's verdict against His people. Note the word **for**. No matter how great the harvest, the issue with God remains.

Verse 1 describes their festival in the present. And all seems well. But Israel should not be deceived by this prosperity. Their future festivals will look very different.

> ²Threshing floor and wine vat shall not feed them,
>   and the new wine shall fail them.
> ³They shall not remain in the land of the LORD,
>   but Ephraim shall return to Egypt,
>   and they shall eat unclean food in Assyria.
> ⁴They shall not pour drink offerings of wine to the LORD,
>   and their sacrifices shall not please him.
> It shall be like mourners' bread to them;
>   all who eat of it shall be defiled;
> for their bread shall be for their hunger only;
>   it shall not come to the house of the LORD.
> ⁵What will you do on the day of the appointed festival,
>   and on the day of the feast of the LORD? (9:2-5)

The exodus is going to go into reverse as the people return to Egypt. **Ephraim shall return to Egypt**. The reference to Egypt is metaphorical. The reality is exile in Assyria. In other words, God's judgment will be exile into Assyria, an exile like a return to slavery in Egypt.

Then what will **the day of the appointed festival** look like? Like a funeral wake. They will not be able to offer sacrifices in the temple, so their festive food will be unclean (9:3, 5), like the funeral food. A dead body in a house made all who ate there unclean. That was not a problem when you could go to the temple and be cleansed. But in exile away from the temple you would remain unclean.

> For behold, they are going away from destruction;
>   but Egypt shall gather them;

Memphis shall bury them.
Nettles shall possess their precious things of silver;
   thorns shall be in their tents. (9:6)

Egypt will gather them, that is, it will capture them and
become a cemetery to them. Again Hosea is talking about exile
in Assyria, but saying it will be like a reversal of the exodus.

Who wants to proclaim, **Rejoice not?** (9:1). Who wants to
be a killjoy? But what if disaster is looming? 'Leave the party'
could be the words of a killjoy, but not if the venue is on
fire. Few people like to warn of God's coming judgment. But
it is the loving thing to do. It is hard to get people to think
about God's judgment when everything is going well. It was
hard for Hosea. It was hard for Peter. Peter talks about people
who mock the notion of a coming judgment because life is
currently so good (2 Pet. 3:3-5). But he says they overlook
two things (2 Pet. 3:5, 8). First, God has a track record. God
has already destroyed the earth when He flooded the world
during the time of Noah. And He will do so again, only this
time through fire (2 Pet. 3:5-7). Second, 'with the Lord one
day is as a thousand years, and a thousand years as one day'
(2 Pet. 3:8). We might think judgment is slow in coming, but
God is being 'patient towards you, not wishing that any should
perish, but that all should reach repentance' (2 Pet. 3:9).

The days of punishment have come;
   the days of recompense have come;
   Israel shall know it.
The prophet is a fool;
   the man of the spirit is mad,
because of your great iniquity
   and great hatred.
[8]The prophet is the watchman of Ephraim with my God;
   yet a fowler's snare is on all his ways,
   and hatred in the house of his God.
[9]They have deeply corrupted themselves
   as in the days of Gibeah:
he will remember their iniquity;
   he will punish their sins. (9:7-9)

The words **punishment** and **punish** at the beginning of
verse 7 and end of verse 9 bracket these verses. These verses

could mean the community is attacking the prophet Hosea. This is what the NIV suggests: **Because your sins are so many and your hostility so great, the prophet is considered a fool, the inspired person a maniac.** Or this verse could mean Hosea is attacking another prophet or prophets. This is how the ESV translates it: **The prophet is a fool; the man of the spirit is mad.** In either case, the people are refusing to hear God's Word. In the case of the NIV's reading, the rejection of God's Word is symbolised by the ill-treatment of prophets. In the case of the ESV's reading, the people are rejecting God's Word in favour of the false prophets whom Hosea attacks. (The ESV is probably preferable as it avoids the need in the NIV to switch the line order to make the argument make sense.) Verse 8 then becomes sarcastic. The prophet is supposed to be a watchman, but he cannot protect the people. The snares that await **on all his paths** describes how all Israel's various attempts to find peace and prosperity apart from God will end in disaster.

As a result, the nation is in **deep** trouble (9:9). Jesus alludes to 9:7 in Luke 21:22: 'for these are days of vengeance, to fulfil all that is written.' The destruction of Jerusalem at the hands of the Romans in A.D. 70 will be another fulfilment of the punishment described by Hosea.

A watchman keeps a lookout for an invading enemy. But what if God is your enemy? It is God's prophets who were supposed to be watchmen against God's advance (9:8; Jer. 6:17; Ezek. 3:17; 33:7; Micah 7:4). But that makes God a strange enemy. He is an enemy who warns of His own coming. He refuses to launch a surprise attack. Instead, He warns us to repent and escape.

Throughout this section, Hosea highlights the way the story of the exodus will go into reverse:

- **God set His people free, but now the people enslave themselves** (8:8-10). 'They have sold themselves among the nations' (8:10). This is the fulfilment of the closing words of the covenant curses in Deuteronomy: 'there you shall offer yourselves for sale to your enemies as male and female slaves' (Deut. 28:68).

- God took His people from Egypt, but now the people
  will return to Egypt (8:13-14). 'They shall return to
  Egypt' (8:13). Egypt shall gather them; Memphis shall
  bury them (9:6). Egypt was a symbol for slavery in foreign
  hands. This time round, though, it will not be Egypt, but
  Assyria who enslaves the people. Assyria is the new
  Egypt. This parallel is clear in 9:3: They will not remain
  in the LORD's land; Ephraim will return to Egypt and
  eat unclean food in Assyria.

- God led His people from the wilderness to an abundant
  land, but now the land will become a wilderness. 'Their
  treasures of silver will be taken over by briers, and
  thorns will overrun their tents' (9:6b).

The Bible story goes into reverse because Israel will return to
slavery like the slavery of Egypt. The exodus will be undone.
Israel will be homeless. Now this theme of the story going
into reverse comes centre stage.

> Like grapes in the wilderness,
>   I found Israel.
> Like the first fruit on the fig tree in its first season,
>   I saw your fathers.
> But they came to Baal-peor
>   and consecrated themselves to the thing of shame,
>   and became detestable like the thing they loved. (9:10)

If the story were a movie, it would open with a beautiful
panning shot in rich colours, with God discovering a grape-
filled oasis in the wilderness. Then the picture would switch
to a spring morning and new fruit on a fig tree. Grapes in the
wilderness is a symbol of the unexpected, perhaps an oasis.
Even if you are not a gardener or farmer, you can imagine
the excitement of seeing the first fruits of a coming harvest,
especially in an agrarian society. Both images capture God's
delight in His people.

But soon everything went wrong. The first half of the verse
describes the first love between God and His bride, Israel. The
'but' at the beginning of the next line signals how tragically
this relationship will break down. The story of Baal Peor is
told in Numbers 25. Israel had been rescued from slavery in

Egypt. Balak, the king of Moab, feared the threat posed by this new nation that was now encamped on his doorstep. So at first he hired Balaam to curse Israel. But Balaam could speak only what God allowed, so in fact he blessed Israel (Num. 22–24; Deut. 23:3-5; Josh. 24:9-10; Neh. 13:2). Balaam then tried another approach, which tragically was more successful. He advised Balak to send Moabite women to seduce the men of Israel and involve them in the worship of Baal (Num. 25:1-9; 31:16). The place where this happened was Peor. God had rescued His people from Egypt so that they might know Him and worship Him. But now instead they are knowing the Moabite women and worshipping Baal. As a result, they **became detestable like the thing they loved** (9:10). Psalm 115:8 echoes this theme: 'Those who make them become like them; so do all who trust in them.'

At Baal Peor 24,000 Israelites died of plague under God's judgment. What would happen now that Israel was again worshipping Baal? In answer to this question, the reversal story reaches it dreadful conclusion.

> [11]Ephraim's glory shall fly away like a bird –
>> no birth, no pregnancy, no conception!
> [12]Even if they bring up children,
>> I will bereave them till none is left.
> Woe to them
>> when I depart from them!
> [13]Ephraim, as I have seen, was like a young palm planted in
> a meadow;
>> but Ephraim must lead his children out to slaughter.

The glory of Ephraim (another term for Israel) in verse 11 is her children. The glory of Ephraim contrasts with its shame in verse 10. Its glory is the children with which God has blessed her. Its shame is their worship of Baal. As a result of that choice to go after shame, there will be no more glory. And that means there will be no more children: **no birth, no pregnancy, no conception** (9:11). Those who are born will be slaughtered (9:12-13): **Even though they give birth, I will put their beloved children to death** (9:16). They will disappear like a flock of birds departing (9:11). In chapter 2, Hosea metaphorically described God's judgment on Israel as the stripping naked of an adulterous wife (2:3). Now he warns that Israel will be stripped of all her glory – her king, her wealth, her children and her relationship with God.

In chapter 8, God promised no fertility in the field, and any produce will be destroyed by a foreign army. Hosea 8:7 says: 'The standing grain has no heads; it shall yield no flour; if it were to yield, strangers would devour it.' Now in the same way, chapter 9 promises no fertility *in the womb,* and any progeny that is produced will be destroyed by a foreign army. It is a terrible picture of the coming destruction of the northern kingdom of Israel. It will be wiped out of the story.

> Give them, O LORD –
> what will you give?
> Give them a miscarrying womb
> and dry breasts. (9:14)

In verse 14, Hosea says: **'Give them, O LORD – what will you give?'** Hosea seems to pause in his prayer. 'Give them …' What should God give them? What should Hosea ask for? He asks for adversity because this might lead to repentance. In the same way, we can pray, 'Lord, please deliver our loved ones from adversity. *Or* use it to strengthen their faith or lead them to Christ.'

> [15]Every evil of theirs is in Gilgal;
> there I began to hate them.
> Because of the wickedness of their deeds
> I will drive them out of my house.
> I will love them no more;
> all their princes are rebels.
> [16]Ephraim is stricken;
> their root is dried up;
> they shall bear no fruit.
> Even though they give birth,
> I will put their beloved children to death.
> [17]My God will reject them
> because they have not listened to him;
> they shall be wanderers among the nations.

What is the crime? Verse 15 says: **Every evil of theirs is in Gilgal; there I began to hate them.** Gilgal was where Saul became Israel's first king. 'So all the people went to Gilgal, and there they made Saul king before the LORD in Gilgal' (1 Sam. 11:15). When the people first ask for a king, the prophet Samuel takes it personally. But God says to him: 'it is not you they have rejected, but they have rejected me as their king' (1 Sam. 8:7). The appointment of Saul at Gilgal was the physical embodiment of Israel's rejection of God as king. That is why 'every evil of theirs is in Gilgal.' Every sin is an act of rebellion against the rule or kingship of God. In that first rejection of God's kingship were the seeds of every subsequent evil. But Gilgal tells in miniature the story of all humanity. We might just as well say, 'Every evil of humanity is in Eden.' All sin stems from the original rejection of God's rule by Adam in the Garden of Eden.

God led His people from wandering in the wilderness into the Promised Land. Now He will drive them out of the Promised Land (9:15) back to wandering in the wilderness (9:17). The language of driving people out of the land is not new in the Bible story. God had promised that He would drive out the Canaanite inhabitants of the land so that He could give it to Israel. He says, for example, in Exodus 33:2: 'I will send an angel before you, and I will drive out the Canaanites, the Amorites, the Hittites, the Perizzites, the Hivites, and the Jebusites.' (See also Exod. 23:28-30; 34:11.) But, in a terrible twist, God will now drive out His own people.

The story of salvation is going into reverse (see 8:13 and 9:3). The story began in verse 10 in the wilderness. That is where God found Israel. There He loved her, prospered her and gave her the land. But the story ends in verse 17 with Israel back in the wilderness, wandering among the nations.

The exodus renewed

The good news is that Hosea 9 is not the end of the story. To understand what happens next in the story and how hope emerges out of judgment, we need to understand who Jesus is. Jesus is God. He is Immanuel, God with us. But He is also us. He is also humanity. Jesus is God's people. Indeed, Jesus is the *true* people of God.

The prophets speak of a faithful remnant, the people within Israel who remain faithful to God. The nation as a whole may be unfaithful and heading for judgment. But some people remain faithful and they will be saved. They are the true people of God. But in the story of Jesus, the faithful remnant comes down to just one person, to Jesus. On the night that He was betrayed, His disciples all betrayed Him or denied Him or fled in fear. There was no one left, except Jesus.

It is a graphic demonstration that in the end only Jesus is truly faithful. None of us has kept God's law as we should. None of us has trusted God as we should. None of us has obeyed God as we should. None of us has worshipped God as we should. None of us – except Jesus. In the end, the faithful remnant is just one person, Jesus.

In Jesus, the reversal of the exodus reaches its climax. In Jesus, the exile reaches its darkest moment. In Jesus, the curses of the climax are poured out in full. The One who is faithful and deserves only the blessings of the covenant takes on Himself the curses of the covenant. God's judgment falls on Jesus in our place.

This section of Hosea closes with these words: **My God will reject them because they have not obeyed him; they will be wanderers among the nations** (9:17). On the cross, God did reject His people in the person of His Son. 'And at the ninth hour Jesus cried out in a loud voice, "Eloi, Eloi, lama sabachthani?" – which means, "My God, my God, why have you forsaken me?"' (Mark 15:34).

The reversal of the story reaches its climax at the cross. Instead of blessing, there is curse. Instead of a land of promise, there is a land of darkness. Instead of milk and honey, there is thirst. Instead of family, there is separation.

In Galatians 3:10, Paul writes: 'For all who rely on works of the law are under a curse; for it is written, "Cursed be everyone who does not abide by all things written in the Book of the Law, and do them."' It is a quote from Deuteronomy 27:26 – from the midst of the covenant curses. Everyone who does not keep God's covenant will be cursed. They will experience the reversal of the exodus, and exile from God.

But Paul goes on: 'Christ redeemed us from the curse of the law by becoming a curse for us – for it is written, "Cursed is everyone who is hanged on a tree" – so that in Christ Jesus the blessing of Abraham might come to the Gentiles, so that we might receive the promised Spirit through faith' (Gal. 3:13-14).

Jesus experienced the full extent of the exodus reversed and the curse of exile. And as a result He accomplished a new exodus, the true exodus. Jesus is the ultimate Passover Lamb who rescued us from slavery to sin and death, and brings us home to a new creation in the presence of God. He puts the story back on track. He endured the judgment we deserved so that we can enjoy the promised ending of the story – to come home to God and be part of His family.

We are homeward bound. Gather up all your best thoughts and images of home. That is our future in Christ. Jesus left His home. He left His Father's side. He became the man with nowhere to lay his head. He died in darkness, abandoned and alone. He did all this so that we could come home. So we could be at home with God. 1 Peter 1:17-19 says:

> Since you call on a Father who judges each person's work impartially, live out your time as foreigners here in reverent fear. For you know that it was not with perishable things such as silver or gold that you were redeemed from the empty way of life handed down to you from your forefathers, but with the precious blood of Christ, a lamb without blemish or defect. (NIV)

Peter is clearly using the language of exodus and Passover. Jesus is the Passover Lamb who has redeemed or liberated us from sin and death. This, as we have seen, is the direction that Hosea 9 points us in. This is where the story leads.

But Peter begins this statement with 'For'. 'For you know that …' The new exodus of Jesus is given as a reason. A reason for what? The answer is Peter's call to live as foreigners. In other words, we are to live as people whose home is somewhere else.

We are not building a home. We are not like the first settlers in the U.S.A. who trekked westward in search of a new home, building a new life from nothing. We have been given a home. We are much more like the generation that settled the land under Joshua. God has fought for us and given us a home. Nehemiah 9:24-25 says:

> So the descendants went in and possessed the land, and you subdued before them the inhabitants of the land, the Canaanites, and gave them into their hand, with their kings and the peoples of the land, that they might do with them as they would. And they captured fortified cities and a rich land,

and took possession of houses full of all good things, cisterns already hewn, vineyards, olive orchards and fruit trees in abundance. So they ate and were filled and became fat and delighted themselves in your great goodness.

Jesus has won a home for us, a home which is already 'full of good things'. We do not have to win it and we do not have to work for it.

But we are to live as those who are homeward bound. Our home is no longer in this world. Our home is now waiting for us in heaven (1 Pet. 1:4). We live in this world like foreigners. We can seek first God's kingdom because our home is glorious and secure and waiting for us.

Jesus says: 'Do not store up for yourselves treasures on earth, where moth and rust destroy, and where thieves break in and steal. But store up for yourselves treasures in heaven, where moth and rust do not destroy, and where thieves do not break in and steal' (Matt. 6:19–20). The tragedy is that many Christians live for the treasures of this passing age. And it is a tragedy. Wealth does not satisfy. Adverts promise satisfaction, but they are, in fact, designed to create dissatisfaction. Wealth corrodes. It is fragile and fleeting. 'Moth and rust destroy, and … thieves break in and steal.' It is like sand slipping through our fingers.

In an essay entitled 'Ash Heap Lives', Francis Schaeffer describes how each week as a boy he would go for a walk. But to get to the countryside he had to walk past the city dump. 'It was a place of junk, fire, stench,' he says. 'Even as a boy I realised that I saw there almost everything people spend their money for. That was where their investment ended.' He goes on:

> Death is a thief. Five minutes after we die, our most treasured possessions which are invested in this life are absolutely robbed from us … In our culture nothing has exhibited such folly more than our automobiles. Go to a showroom and see the pride with which a man drives out his new car. Then think of an automobile graveyard or a rusting, stripped, junked car, abandoned on a city street. They are shells screaming out tremendous sermons against all practical materialism: 'You're fools! You're fools! You're fools!' And Christians – as well as any others – can be such fools with their wealth.[1]

---

1.   Francis Schaeffer, 'Ash Heap Lives', available online. (Originally published in Francis Schaeffer, *Ash Heap Lives*, Norfolk Press, 1975.)

We are pilgrims in this world, foreigners, strangers (Heb. 11:13-16; 1 Pet. 2:11). This world as it is now is not our home. We pass through life looking ahead to something bigger and better. One day this earth will be a 'home of righteousness' (2 Pet. 3:13), but only when we arrive at a heavenly version of this earth; only when this earth comes under a new regime; only when Christ is at the centre and His glory fills the horizons.

STUDY QUESTIONS

1. What images does home evoke for you?

2. People who worship idols 'became detestable like the thing they loved' (Hosea 9:10; Ps. 115:8). Where can you see this principle at work today?

3. Why is God a strange kind of enemy?

4. Identify examples from your experience of praying that God might use adversity rather than remove it.

5. How does Jesus put the story of God's people back on track?

6. What does it mean for us to live with the new creation as our home?

7. Think about big life decisions you have made or are making now. It might be things to do with your job or your home or your relationships. What would it mean to make those decisions in light of your home in heaven?

Questions for Personal Reflection

1. What is that you love and trust? How might you become like them?

2. What did you do yesterday for your present comfort or security? What did you do yesterday for God's future?

3. What will you do tomorrow to store up treasure on earth? What will you do tomorrow to store up treasure in heaven?

4. Death separates us from every source of happiness except Jesus. Can you say with Paul that 'to die is gain' (Phil. 1:21) because Jesus is your ultimate joy?

9

God Predicts a Harvest
(Hosea 10:1-15)

Many books have been written to help Christians cope with adversity. That is clearly understandable. Suffering is part of life in a fallen world. And it does throw into question the power and love of God. That is true at a philosophical level as people ask, 'How can a God of love allow suffering?' But it is also true at a deeply personal level as people ask, 'How can my God of love allow my suffering?' Adversity is a threat to faith.

Rather fewer books have been written to help Christians cope with prosperity. Yet from the Bible's perspective prosperity is as much a threat to faith as adversity. As Israel stood on the verge of the Promised Land, for example, Moses warned them of the dangers of prosperity:

> So you shall keep the commandments of the LORD your God by walking in his ways and by fearing him. For the LORD your God is bringing you into a good land, a land of brooks of water, of fountains and springs, flowing out in the valleys and hills, a land of wheat and barley, of vines and fig trees and pomegranates, a land of olive trees and honey, a land in which you will eat bread without scarcity, in which you will lack nothing, a land whose stones are iron, and out of whose hills you can dig copper. And you shall eat and be full, and you shall bless the LORD your God for the good land he has given you.

> Take care lest you forget the LORD your God by not keep-
> ing his commandments and his rules and his statutes, which
> I command you today, lest, when you have eaten and are full
> and have built good houses and live in them, and when your
> herds and flocks multiply and your silver and gold is multi-
> plied and all that you have is multiplied, then your heart be
> lifted up, and you forget the LORD your God, who brought
> you out of the land of Egypt, out of the house of slavery
> (Deut. 8:6-14).

Moses goes on to remind the people how the LORD led them
through the wilderness and provided for them along the way.
He concludes: 'Beware lest you say in your heart, "My power
and the might of my hand have gotten me this wealth." You
shall remember the LORD your God, for it is he who gives
you power to get wealth' (Deut. 8:17-18).

We find a similar picture in Luke's Gospel where Jesus
repeatedly warns about the dangers of wealth. It is striking
just how often Luke includes these warnings. This, it would
seem, is the main threat to faithful discipleship:

- 'And he lifted up his eyes on his disciples, and said:
  "Blessed are you who are poor, for yours is the kingdom of
  God … But woe to you who are rich, for you have received
  your consolation."' (Luke 6:20, 24)

- 'And as for what fell among the thorns, they are those who
  hear, but as they go on their way they are choked by the
  cares and riches and pleasures of life, and their fruit does
  not mature.' (Luke 8:14)

- 'And he said to them, "Take care, and be on your guard
  against all covetousness, for one's life does not consist
  in the abundance of his possessions." And he told them
  a parable, saying, "The land of a rich man produced
  plentifully …"' (Luke 12:15-21)

- 'And he said to his disciples, "Therefore I tell you, do not be
  anxious about your life, what you will eat, nor about your
  body, what you will put on … Instead, seek his kingdom,
  and these things will be added to you."' (Luke 12:22-31)

- 'Sell your possessions, and give to the needy. Provide
  yourselves with money bags that do not grow old, with

a treasure in the heavens that does not fail, where no thief approaches and no moth destroys. For where your treasure is, there will your heart be also.' (Luke 12:33-34)

- 'So therefore, any one of you who does not renounce all that he has cannot be my disciple.' (Luke 14:33)

- 'I tell you, use worldly wealth to gain friends for yourselves, so that when it is gone, you will be welcomed into eternal dwellings.' (Luke 16:9, NIV)

- '"No servant can serve two masters, for either he will hate the one and love the other, or he will be devoted to the one and despise the other. You cannot serve God and money." The Pharisees, who were lovers of money, heard all these things, and they ridiculed him.' (Luke 16:13-14)

- 'Jesus, looking at him with sadness, said, "How difficult it is for those who have wealth to enter the kingdom of God! For it is easier for a camel to go through the eye of a needle than for a rich person to enter the kingdom of God."' (Luke 18:24-25)

The writer of Proverbs sums it up neatly when he says:

> Give me neither poverty nor riches;
>> feed me with the food that is needful for me,
> lest I be full and deny you
>> and say, 'Who is the LORD?'
> or lest I be poor and steal
>> and profane the name of my God. (Prov. 30:8-9)

Hosea 10 is another contribution to this theme. It, too, is a warning about the dangers of prosperity. But Hosea 10 provides its warning in the form of a worked example. This is a case study drawn from Israel's history. The theme is established in the opening verse: **Israel is a luxuriant vine that yields its fruit** (10:1). Israel is enjoying a period of luxury with abundant harvests. What happens when a nation enjoys prosperity? What happens when prosperity leads God's people into unfaithfulness?

A nation with no fruit (10:1-2)

> ¹Israel is a luxuriant vine
>   that yields its fruit.
> The more his fruit increased,
>   the more altars he built;
> as his country improved,
>   he improved his pillars.
> ²Their heart is false;
>   now they must bear their guilt.
> The LORD will break down their altars
>   and destroy their pillars.

In 9:10, Hosea says that when God first found Israel, that is, when He first formed her as a nation, she was 'like grapes in the wilderness'. Now Hosea winds forward in the story to a time when Israel has become a luxuriant vine spreading through the promised land. Psalm 80 uses similar imagery. It describes how God 'brought a vine out of Egypt'. He cleared the ground for it by driving the nations out of the Promised Land. Under God's care it has prospered and had now 'sent out its branches to the sea' (Ps. 80:8-11).

Hosea's ministry began during a period of expansion and prosperity. The reigns of Uzziah in Judah and Jeroboam II in Israel, where Hosea was ministering, were a time of peace and economic growth. But instead of thanking God for its prosperity, Israel has used its wealth to build altars to other gods. Indeed, there is a direct correlation between her growing prosperity and her growing apostasy. **The more his fruit increased, the more altars he built**. These are not altars to the worship of the LORD (as the following line makes clear). **As his country improved, he improved his pillars**. The 'pillars' here are standing stones or something akin to totem poles – shrines to other gods, possibly local fertility symbols. Worship in Israel should have been centralised in Jerusalem. This proliferation of local centres of worship was leading to a proliferation of false worship. Their material prosperity has not led the people to give thanks to the LORD for His provision. Instead, their **heart is false**. The people give the credit to others gods. As a result, **the LORD will break down their altars and destroy their pillars**. They have invested their prosperity in altars and pillars, but these same altars and pillars will be destroyed by the LORD.

Israel is a nation bearing lots of fruit. But it is not the fruit that really matters. Her harvests are good. But, as we shall see, the harvest that really matters is absent – the harvest of covenant love which is reaped from the sowing of righteousness. **Sow for yourselves righteousness; reap steadfast love** (10:12). That is the invitation of this chapter. The present reality is in stark contrast: **You have ploughed iniquity; you have reaped injustice; you have eaten the fruit of lies** (10:13). The headline news in Israel was of another good harvest. But behind the headlines, says Hosea, the real story is of a very different harvest. The iniquity that the people have sown will lead to a harvest of judgment.

A political system with no integrity (10:3-4)
The planting of iniquity and the harvesting of injustice is the metaphor. What is the reality to which it points? Hosea says it is a picture of both the political and religious systems of Israel.

> ³For now they will say:
>   'We have no king,
> for we do not fear the LORD;
>   and a king – what could he do for us?'
> ⁴They utter mere words;
>   with empty oaths they make covenants;
> so judgment springs up like poisonous weeds
>   in the furrows of the field.

Hosea looks to a time when Israel has no king – or at least no functional king. The people have lost confidence in the political system. So they would have no hope even if they did have a king. **What could [a king] do for us?**, the people cry, just as today people ask, 'What do politicians ever do for us?'

At first sight, the phrase **judgment springs up like poisonous weeds** in verse 4 looks a strange phrase. Why would judgment be poisonous? The NIV translation gives us a clue. It reads **lawsuits spring up like poisonous weeds**. Lawyers have little to do when people operate with trust and integrity. If you sow integrity, then you will reap a culture of trust without much need for recourse to law. But if you sow iniquity, then you will reap a culture of mistrust and betrayal in which lawsuits will abound. **They utter mere words**, Hosea says. In other words, their words have no power. They do not correspond to a genuine commitment. **With empty oaths they make covenants**. When they do make contracts, those contracts cannot be trusted. The promises these covenants enshrine are empty promises. As a result, **lawsuits spring up like poisonous weeds**.

It is the same today. Since 1801, the motto of the London Stock Exchange has been 'my word is my bond' (in Latin 'dictum meum pactum'). Originally deals were made without the use of written documents. But today lawyers in large companies earn big money drawing up and enforcing contracts. It is the same with marriage. When people are faithful to their marriage covenant, there is little recourse to law. But today divorce suits are commonplace. All too often, the result is misery for those involved and trauma for their children. **Lawsuits spring up like poisonous weeds**.

A religious system with no future (10:5-8)

> [5]The inhabitants of Samaria tremble
>   for the calf of Beth-aven.
> Its people mourn for it, and so do its idolatrous priests –
>   those who rejoiced over it and over its glory –
>   for it has departed from them.
> [6]The thing itself shall be carried to Assyria
>   as tribute to the great king.
> Ephraim shall be put to shame,
>   and Israel shall be ashamed of his idol.
> [7]Samaria's king shall perish
>   like a twig on the face of the waters.
> [8]The high places of Aven, the sin of Israel,
>   shall be destroyed.
> Thorn and thistle shall grow up
>   on their altars,
> and they shall say to the mountains, Cover us,
>   and to the hills, Fall on us.

Nearly two centuries before Hosea, King Rehoboam had succeeded his father Solomon to the throne. Following the advice of his young counsellors, he had intensified the enforced labour that Solomon had initiated. The result was a rebellion led by Jeroboam. The ten northern tribes split away from the two southern tribes of Judah and Benjamin, who remained loyal to the dynasty of David.

Jeroboam became Jeroboam I, the first king of the separate northern kingdom, Israel. Jeroboam, however, was faced with an immediate problem. His subjects were regularly making the pilgrimage to the temple in Jerusalem, right at the heart of the rival regime. That meant money for the southern kingdom of Judah and exposure to their propaganda. So, as we have noted when we looked at 8:5-6, Jeroboam established two rival shrines so that the people did not travel to the temple in Jerusalem (1 Kings 13:26-33). He set up two golden calves, one in the south of his kingdom in Bethel and one in the north in Dan. But by this point in the story the northern shrine has fallen into enemy hands, so only one remains, the calf at Bethel.

This is what Hosea is referring to in verse 5: **The inhabitants of Samaria tremble for the calf of Beth-aven**. Except that Hosea does not refer to it as Bethel. 'Bethel' means 'house of God'. But this is no house of God. Instead, Hosea gives it a nickname. He calls it 'Beth-aven', which means 'house of wickedness'. The house of God has become the home of wickedness.

The irony is that **the inhabitants of Samaria tremble for the calf of Beth-aven**. Samaria is the capital of the northern kingdom of Israel and here it represents the nation as a whole. You should tremble *before* your God. But the people **tremble *for*** their calf. It is a sign of its impotence. It is true that your god should make you fear. But your God should make you fear because of His majesty and holiness. Instead the calf of Beth-aven makes people fear for its safety.

And the people are right to fear for its future because it will be carried away to Assyria (10:6). Again, its impotence is highlighted. It is unable to move of its own accord and has to be carried. It is unable to protect itself (let alone protect the people) and will be carried away. **Departed** in verse 5 is literally 'exiled'. The calf will be exiled.

Hosea presents God's judgment as a series of reversals:

- The bountiful harvests of verse 1 (**Israel is a luxuriant vine that yields its fruit**) will become a harvest of judgment in verse 4 (**judgment springs up like poisonous weeds in the furrows of the field**).

- The glory of Israel in verse 5 (**the calf of Beth-aven**) will become a source of shame in verse 6 as it is carried away (**Ephraim shall be put to shame, and Israel shall be ashamed of his idol**).

- The many altars built in verse 1 (**The more his fruit increased the more altars he built**) will be destroyed in verses 2 and 8 (**The LORD will break down their altars ... The high places of Aven, the sin of Israel, shall be destroyed**).

The thorns growing among the altars in verse 8 are a sign of desolation. There is an area near to where I live, which from any distance looks like a piece of wild woodland. And indeed this is what it is. But upon closer inspection you can trace the outline of broken walls among the undergrowth. Roof slates and bricks lie discarded, along with the odd bit of furniture. Clearly, there used to be houses on the site. But they have long gone. The trees and bushes are a sign of their destruction. So it will be of the religious sites in Israel. Soon they will fade into an undergrowth of thorns and thistles.

But the fate of the people is worse. As the Assyrian army wreaks destruction across the land, the people wish they could die quickly in an earthquake rather than endure the prolonged suffering of slavery. **They shall say to the mountains, Cover us, and to the hills, Fall on us** (10:8). We find this sentiment echoed by Jesus in Luke 23:30 as He looks ahead to the destruction of Jerusalem at the hands of the Romans.

But the fall of Samaria in 722 b.c. and the fall of Jerusalem in a.d. 70 are themselves pointers to the final judgment. In Revelation 6:15-17, we have another echo of Hosea 10:8 in the apostle John's vision of the coming final day:

> Then the kings of the earth and the great ones and the generals and the rich and the powerful, and everyone, slave and free, hid themselves in the caves and among the rocks of the mountains, calling to the mountains and rocks, 'Fall on us

and hide us from the face of him who is seated on the throne, and from the wrath of the Lamb, for the great day of their wrath has come, and who can stand?'

Israel's judgment is a pointer to the judgment of all humanity. In that day, people will again wish for a quick death rather than face God's wrath. In that day, 'who can stand?'

But there is hope. In the book of Revelation, the apostle John goes on to say: 'Then I saw another angel ascending from the rising of the sun, with the seal of the living God, and he called with a loud voice to the four angels who had been given power to harm earth and sea, saying, "Do not harm the earth or the sea or the trees, until we have sealed the servants of our God on their foreheads"' (Rev. 7:2-3). We are sealed through faith in the gospel message. Paul describes the Holy Spirit as a seal given to those who believe. 'In [Christ] you also, when you heard the word of truth, the gospel of your salvation, and believed in him, were sealed with the promised Holy Spirit, who is the guarantee of our inheritance until we acquire possession of it, to the praise of his glory' (Eph. 1:13-14). The Spirit is a sign that God's wrath will not touch us.

A history doomed to be repeated (10:9-10)

⁹From the days of Gibeah, you have sinned, O Israel;
    there they have continued.
Shall not the war against the unjust overtake them in Gibeah?
¹⁰When I please, I will discipline them,
    and nations shall be gathered against them
    when they are bound up for their double iniquity.

Gibeah was the scene of one of the most sordid episodes in Israel's long history of wickedness. It is one story children are never taught in Sunday school. In the days of the judges, a Levite was travelling with his concubine. That a Levite, one of the tribe entrusted with the care of Israel's worship, has a concubine is bad enough. But worse is to follow. They need to stop for the night and the Levite's servant suggests they stop in a Jebusite village. The Jebusites were Gentiles. So the Levite decides they should press on to Gibeah in the tribe of Benjamin where, he supposes, they will be safely welcomed by fellow Israelites. He could not have been more wrong.

At first, no one offers them hospitality. Finally, an old man welcomes them into his home. But, during the night, wicked men from the city surround the house. 'Bring out the man who came into your house,' they demand, 'that we may know him' (Judg. 19:22). In other words, they want to gang-rape the guest. The old man rightly says they are acting 'wickedly' and describes their request as a 'vile' and an 'outrageous thing' (Judg. 19:23-24). But then he himself offers his daughter and the Levite's concubine as an alternative. The men continue their demands until the Levite pushes his concubine out to them and the men of the city, we are told, 'abused her all night' (Judg. 19:25).

In the morning, the Levite opens the door of the house. 'Behold, there was his concubine lying at the door of the house, with her hands on the threshold' (Judg. 19:27). He callously tells her to get up because it is time to leave. But she is dead. He clearly has no love for her. To him, she is simply a possession, to be used and abused and disposed of as he sees fit. But he is affronted at the violation of his property. So he cuts up her body into twelve pieces and posts them to the twelve tribes of Israel, calling on them to do justice. When the people of Israel hear what has happened they say, 'Such a thing has never happened or been seen from the day that the people of Israel came up out of the land of Egypt until this day; consider it, take counsel, and speak' (Judg. 19:30).

The tribes of Israel gather together and demand that the tribe of Benjamin hand over the men of Gibeah. The Benjaminites refuse and the result is civil war. Eventually, Israel prevails, and the Benjaminites are massacred. Twenty-five thousand Benjaminite men are killed, leaving only 600 survivors. Once their bloodlust is satiated, the people of Israel begin to realise the consequences. 'They lifted up their voices and wept bitterly. And they said, "O Lord, the God of Israel, why has this happened in Israel, that today there should be one tribe lacking in Israel?"' (Judg. 21:2-3). The tribe of Benjamin just about survives. But the twelve tribes of Israel came perilously close to becoming merely the eleven tribes of Israel.

Now this story is about to be repeated. Hosea says, **From the days of Gibeah, you have sinned, O Israel; there they have continued** (10:9). Gibeah's crime was not the exception.

Israel has continued to sin. The events at Gibeah might have been one of the worst incidents, but it was an unrestrained expression of the sin in the hearts of all people. And so Israel has not moved on. **They have continued** with the same patterns of behaviour.

The war against Gibeah was a **war against the unjust**. They had committed crime and it was right that they be punished (even though the execution and the executioners of that justice were flawed). Justice had overtaken them. But now, suggests Hosea, justice will again overtake the unjust. **Shall not the war against the unjust overtake them in Gibeah?** (10:9) **When I please, I will discipline them** (10:10). This time God's instrument of justice will not be the tribes of Israel, but other nations: **Nations shall be gathered against them when they are bound up for their double iniquity** (10:10).

The word **overtaken** hangs in the air, pregnant with terrible resonances. The war against the tribe of Benjamin had all but wiped them out. They had gone from over 25,000 men to just 600. What would happen now if God Himself disciplined the northern kingdom of Israel? Might this lead to them being 'overtaken' and wiped out completely and irrevocably?

Israel the calf (10:11)

> Ephraim was a trained calf
>> that loved to thresh,
>> and I spared her fair neck
> but I will put Ephraim to the yoke;
>> Judah must plough;
>> Jacob must harrow for himself.

Hosea likens Israel to a heifer used for ploughing. In the past, she was well trained and loved her work. In other words, she loved obeying and serving the Lord. **I spared her fair neck** means that in the past God did not let her be treated harshly. But now she must suffer and toil. This is not the yoke that Jesus promises when He says, 'Come to me ... For my yoke is easy, and my burden is light' (Matt. 11:28-30). This is a yoke of judgment. This is being harnessed for servitude at the hands of the Assyrians.

It is Ephraim (or Israel) who will bear this yoke. But Hosea also mentions the southern kingdom of Judah. It is a reminder that the northern tribes of Israel who *heard* Hosea's words were not the only audience. The southern tribes of Judah who *read* Hosea's words were also to take note. The two kingdoms were, in one sense, brothers (literally developing from the twelve sons of Jacob, who was also called Israel). But as often as not after their division into the two kingdoms, they were also rivals and went to war with each other on a number of occasions. So perhaps it was tempting for Judah to rejoice in Israel's exile. But Hosea's references to Judah are a sign that she should see in Israel's fate a warning of her own future if she does not repent. Just as Ephraim will be **put ... to the yoke** so **Judah must plough**. It is a reminder that these words spoken to the northern kingdom of Israel many centuries ago come to all God's people as the voice of God.

Israel the sower (10:12)

> Sow for yourselves righteousness;
>   reap steadfast love;
>   break up your fallow ground,
> for it is the time to seek the LORD,
>   that he may come and rain righteousness upon you.

God has been addressing the people in the first person. But now Hosea speaks to them. In the light of God's warning of judgment, he exhorts the people to act, but also gives to them an implicit promise.

We are still on the farm, but now Israel is likened to a farmer sowing seed. Using this imagery, Hosea exhorts people:

- to sow righteousness

- to break their fallow ground

- to seek the LORD

These are all different ways of making the same point. The people are to seek God in faith and repentance. This idea is expressed in the images of sowing and ploughing.

To **sow for yourselves righteousness** is not simply to do righteous deeds. Righteousness meant doing right by your word or being true to a covenant. That this righteousness is covenantal is confirmed by the corresponding promise of **steadfast love** or covenant love. So to sow righteousness was to return to the covenant that God had made with His people. It meant being loyal to God. It meant using the provision in the covenant for sin, namely the atonement symbolised in sacrifice. The people were to turn from their sin and turn back to God in renewed fidelity and seek the forgiveness that was embodied in the sacrificial system.

Fallow ground is ground that has not been worked. Before it can be fruitful again it must be broken up and that is hard work. So it was with the national culture of Israel. Israel's religious life had fallen into decay. To return to vitality would be hard work. Habits would have to be relearnt. The culture would have to be reset. Above all, they would need to be repentant. Imagine soil from a vegetable patch that has been worked year after year. Compare that with a footpath that has been trodden hard by the passage of many people. The vegetable patch is immediately fruitful. But the path will require a lot of work, breaking the crust, loosening the soil, adding compost. In the same way, the Israelites are to break their hard hearts and seek mercy from God. If sin has become a habit in your life, then change is rarely easy. There is often hard work involved in reforming habits. The hard soil of our instinctive responses and patterns of thinking needs to be broken up. Saying 'No' to sin in these circumstances will often feel like part of us is dying. But that is the language Paul uses to describe our attitude to sin. We are to put it to death (Col. 3:5). Over time, however, new habits of righteousness start to replace the hard soil in our hearts.

A twofold promise accompanies these exhortations. First, if Israel sows righteousness, then they will **reap steadfast love**. If they return to the covenant, then they will enjoy the covenant love of God. Imagine, as Hosea has already invited us to do, an unfaithful wife who has abandoned her husband. If she returns to her marital covenant, then she can expect (if her husband is gracious, and Israel's husband is gracious) to enjoy again covenant love. Second, if Israel sows righteousness, then God **may come and rain righteousness upon you**. The battle with sin is often painful. But it is worth it. It leads to joy.

It leads to the joy of knowing God and knowing ourselves to be in His will. This promise is echoed at the conclusion of the book of Hosea: 'I will be like the dew to Israel ... They shall return and dwell beneath my shadow; they shall flourish like the grain; they shall blossom like the vine; their fame shall be like the wine of Lebanon' (Hosea 14:5, 7).

Paul alludes to these words in 2 Corinthians 9:10-11 where he is exhorting the Corinthians to give generously to the poor in Jerusalem: 'He who supplies seed to the sower and bread for food will supply and multiply your seed for sowing and increase the harvest of your righteousness. You will be enriched in every way for all your generosity, which through us will produce thanksgiving to God.' This is not a promise that we will grow economically wealthy if we give money to God. It is a promise that we will grow *spiritually* wealthy.

Israel the reaper (10:13-15)

> [13]You have ploughed iniquity;
>   you have reaped injustice;
>   you have eaten the fruit of lies.
> Because you have trusted in your own way
>   and in the multitude of your warriors,
> [14]therefore the tumult of war shall arise among your people,
>   and all your fortresses shall be destroyed,
> as Shalman destroyed Beth-arbel on the day of battle;
>   mothers were dashed in pieces with their children.
> [15]Thus it shall be done to you, O Bethel,
>   because of your great evil.
> At dawn the king of Israel
>   shall be utterly cut off.

Hosea calls on Israel to sow righteousness. The problem is Israel has been planting other things. Instead of sowing righteousness, the people have chosen to plough **iniquity** (10:13). Inevitably, this has led to a harvest of **injustice** and **lies** (10:13). Instead of trusting God, they have trusted in their own wisdom and their own military strength (10:13).

The initial harvest is a national life characterised by injustice and lies. But the ultimate harvest is the judgment of God. War will come upon Israel (10:14). History does not record what Shalman did at Beth-arbel (10:14). But Hosea's readers clearly knew about it and it was not good. It appears to be synonymous with Israel's king being **utterly cut off** (10:15). Judgment is coming. But still God warns His people. Still there is time to repent.

Chapter 10 is full of agricultural imagery, in particular the language of sowing and harvesting:

* Israel is producing a lot of literal fruit, so she is reaping big harvests (10:1).

* Israel is not producing spiritual fruit, so she is reaping a harvest of lawsuits (10:4).

* Israel is not producing spiritual fruit, so her religious sites will become unharvested wastelands (10:8).

* If Israel sows covenant faithfulness, then she will reap a harvest of covenant love (10:12)

* Israel is sowing iniquity, so she is reaping a harvest of injustice (10:13).

* Israel is sowing iniquity, so she will reap a harvest of judgment (10:13-14).

The New Testament picks up this theme in two important ways.

Sow to the Spirit – Galatians 6:7-9
In 10:12, Hosea invites Israel to sow righteousness and harvest love. Instead, in 10:13, Israel sows iniquity and harvests injustice. Paul puts a similar invitation to Christians:

> Do not be deceived: God is not mocked, for whatever one sows, that will he also reap. For the one who sows to his own flesh will from the flesh reap corruption, but the one who sows to the Spirit will from the Spirit reap eternal life. And let us not grow weary of doing good, for in due season we will reap, if we do not give up. (Gal. 6:7-9)

'God cannot be mocked,' says Paul, 'a man reaps what he sows.' There is no way to avoid the principle of sowing and harvesting. In the agricultural world, you cannot plant apple pips and expect to harvest pears. You cannot plant peas and expect to reap corn. The same is true in the spiritual world.

You reap what you sow. You cannot neglect the means of grace that God has provided and then expect to harvest good fruit in your life. You cannot indulge your sinful desires and then wonder why you are not becoming more like Jesus. Paul says that those who sow to the sinful nature will reap destruction.

But if you sow to the Spirit, then a different story emerges. Every action is one step towards a habit. The question is: What kind of habit? Is it a habit of the flesh or a habit of the Spirit?

We need to avoid whatever might *provoke* our sinful desires – situations in which we might face temptation. We cannot change ourselves through laws and codes. Change must begin within our hearts. But avoiding temptation does have a part to play. The Bible talks about 'fleeing' temptation. It creates a space for new desires to supplant our sinful desires.

We also need to avoid whatever might *strengthen* our sinful desires. The culture of the world around us celebrates sins and spreads lies about God. We cannot avoid contact with the world entirely. But we can avoid those aspects of the culture that feed the temptations with which we particularly struggle. It might mean not watching late-night television if that feeds our sexual lusts. It might mean not reading glossy magazines if they feed our longing for more possessions. It might mean not watching romantic comedies if that feeds our discontentment in our marriage or with our singleness.

As Hosea and Paul remind us, saying 'No' to the sinful nature is like farming. We need to weed out the sin in our lives. Sometimes weeding out sin in our lives is like pulling up an old tree stump. A particular sin may have gripped our heart for so long that its roots run deep. It has become a habit. Pulling up this weed will be hard and painful. We need to **break up [our] fallow ground** (10:12). It is better to pull up the weeds of sin as soon they emerge when they are small and rootless. But this is a constant task. Every day's neglect makes the job harder.

I once visited the allotment of a friend. One allotment near his was perfectly maintained. There was not a single weed to be seen. The problem was there were also no vegetables. The man who owned this particular allotment was retired. He enjoyed the rhythm of leaving the house in the morning and going to work his allotment. He enjoyed the comradeship it provided with other allotment holders. But he was not much interested in growing vegetables. Every day he busied himself about his allotment without ever planting anything. As a result, his patch had no weeds at all. But it was still completely unfruitful.

To reap a spiritual harvest, we need not only to root out the weeds of sin. We also need to sow to the Spirit. That means implanting the gospel into our hearts and minds. How do we that? By using the means of grace that God has provided: meditating on His Word, worshipping with His people, coming to Him in prayer for help, embedding ourselves in the community of God's people, discipling others and being discipled, feeding on Christ by faith in the Lord's Supper. In all these ways, we implant the seed of the gospel in our lives. And that seed will produce a good harvest. One of the best ways to keep down the weeds in your garden is to ensure there are plenty of good plants to crowd them out. One of the ways to keep down sin in your life is to ensure that the gospel of Jesus is crowding out sin. The more we relish the glory and grace of Christ, the less the temptations of sin will attract us.

Abide in the vine – John 15:1-8

Hosea's description of Israel as a vine echoes a similar image used by the prophet Isaiah. In Isaiah 5:1-7, the prophet describes Israel as God's vineyard (see also Ps. 80:8-16; Isa. 27:2-6; Jer. 2:21; 12:10; Ezek. 15; 17; 19:10-14). But Israel has borne no fruit, so God will uproot her. At first, Hosea looks to be using the imagery in a different way. He describes Israel as a luxuriant vine that produces a lot of fruit. But these literal harvests mask the spiritual barrenness of Israel. Spiritually, the only harvest she is producing are the poisonous weeds of lawsuits (10:4), injustice and lies (10:13).

Jesus picks up this imagery in John 15. He describes Himself as 'the true vine' (John 15:1). He is the true vine in contrast to Israel, the vine that proved false. He is the vine that has produced fruit, that has produced a harvest of righteousness.

Jesus goes on to describe His Father as 'the vine dresser'. 'Every branch of mine that does not bear fruit he takes away, and every branch that does bear fruit he prunes, that it may bear more fruit ... Abide in me, and I in you. As the branch cannot bear fruit by itself, unless it abides in the vine, neither can you, unless you abide in me' (John 15:2, 4). We must remain in Christ and we must expect God to prune us. If we do not remain in Christ, then like Israel in Hosea 10 we can expect God to uproot us.

The picture here is of Jesus as a vine, a long stem off of which are hundreds of branches representing Christians. Jesus gives us life – just as the stem of a vine gives life to the branches. Cut off a branch and it soon withers. Without Jesus, the branches have no life. But connected to Him, they bear good fruit.

This picture helps us understand the relationship between salvation and our actions. The message of Isaiah, Hosea and Jesus is *not* that we must try hard to produce a good harvest so that we can earn salvation. It is not a pull-yourselves-up-by-your-bootstraps philosophy of life. If Hosea 10 leaves us frustrated at our inability to produce a harvest, then it is so that we run into the arms of Jesus. We need a Saviour.

Jesus is the true Vine and He is the One who gives life to the branches. That is how it is with trees. Branches do not get life from their fruit. Vines do not draw life back out of their grapes. No, they get their life from the stem. But how do you know which branches are alive? By their fruit. Fruit is a sure sign of life. But it is not the cause of life.

So it is with the Christian. Fruit (in the form of spiritual growth, knowledge of God expressed in prayer, love for others, a longing to spread the name of Jesus, a desire to meet with God's people, a hunger for His Word, good works) is a sure sign of spiritual life. This fruit shows that we belong to Christ, that we are genuine Christians, that we are connected to the stem. But they do not give us life – no more than grapes give life to the vine. The life comes from the stem. Our life comes from Jesus

That is why we can say, 'Without fruit, you cannot be a Christian.' But at the same time we say, 'We are not saved by what we do, but only through the life that Jesus gives.' The fruit does not make you a Christian, but it does show that you are a Christian. Jesus says: 'By this my Father is glorified, that you bear much fruit and so prove to be my disciples' (John 15:8).

In John 15, Jesus is talking about fruitfulness. In verse 16, He says: 'You did not choose me, but I chose you and appointed you that you should go and bear fruit and that your fruit should abide.' The purpose of Jesus for us is that we produce fruit. He chose us and set us apart to be fruitful. And that fruit is fruit that will last. It is the fruit of godliness, service and mission.

So how can we be fruitful? What is the secret of effective Christian living?

First, God Himself is at work. We cannot be fruitful on our own. We have a part to play, as we shall see. But we are dependent on God. Jesus says: 'Every branch that does bear fruit he prunes, that it may bear more fruit. Already you are clean because of the word that I have spoken to you' (John 15:2-3). I have already said that we are to weed out sin in our lives. The metaphor shifts slightly here to that of pruning out dead wood. But the meaning is the same. This time, however, God takes the lead. He uses the circumstances of our lives to shape us for service. God also makes us fit for purpose through His Word. The words 'prune' and 'clean' are the same word in Greek. God cleans us through the circumstances of our lives and He cleans us through His Word. The Word of God identifies where we are being unfruitful. It highlights the sin that makes us fruitless. And the Word of God gives the remedy in the work of Jesus – His power, His forgiveness, His grace. It motivates us to holiness when we are lacklustre. It shapes our lives and forms our character.

Our responsibility is to remain in Christ. 'Abide in me, and I in you. As the branch cannot bear fruit by itself, unless it abides in the vine, neither can you, unless you abide in me. I am the vine; you are the branches. Whoever abides in me and I in him, he it is that bears much fruit, for apart from me you can do nothing' (John 15:4-5). A branch cannot become disconnected from the stem of the vine and continue to bear fruit. It will just wither and die. In the same way, we can only be fruitful if we remain in Christ. Bearing fruit is not humanly possible. It is the work of Christ in us. Without continual dependence upon Jesus – without communing with Him, talking to Him in prayer, seeking the grace that is found through Him, looking to the resources He supplies, submitting to his will – fruitfulness is impossible.

'Remaining in Christ' can seem a bit vague. It can seem a bit mystical – as if only monks and nuns can really do it. But Jesus defines it for us and it actually turns out to be very down to earth. 'If you keep my commandments, you will abide in my love, just as I have kept my Father's commandments and abide in his love' (John 15:10). It is about day-to-day obedience to the word of Jesus because we enjoy His love. This is not simply about adhering to a list of dos and don'ts. This obedience springs from a relationship of love. 'As the Father has loved me, so have I loved you. Abide in my love. If you keep my commandments, you will abide in my love, just as I have kept my Father's commandments and abide in his love.' (John 15:9-10) Love and obedience are all tied up together. Love leads to obedience, and obedience is all about loving (John 14:15, 21, 23). Love expresses itself in obedience, and obedience express itself in love.

It is obedience that leads to joy. 'These things I have spoken to you, that my joy may be in you, and that your joy may be full' (John 15:11). Remaining in Jesus and obeying His words is not a stoical act in which we grit our teeth and get on with it. This is the way in which Jesus gives us joy:

> Sow for yourselves righteousness;
>   reap steadfast love;
>   break up your fallow ground,
> for it is the time to seek the LORD,
>   that he may come and rain righteousness upon you. (10:12)

What did you sow yesterday? What did you allow to influence you? What harvest will it produce in your life?

What will you sow today? What will you reap tomorrow?

Verse 13 says: **Because you have trusted in your own way.** What tasks or struggles await you today? This week? How will you overcome them? How will you remain godly? Ask God to empower you by His Spirit to live for Him.

Study Questions

1. What are some of the dangers of prosperity?

2. Identify examples from your experience of these dangers.

3. Identify positive examples from your experience of reaping what you sow.

4. Identify negative examples from your experience of reaping what you sow.

5. How might we sow to the flesh?

6. How can we sow to the Spirit?

7. What does it mean to remain in Christ?

Questions for Personal Reflection

1. Are you trying to break the law of sowing and reaping? Are you sowing to the flesh and then wondering why your struggle with sin is so difficult or wondering why you are not seeing a good harvest in your life?

2. What do you need to do to avoid provoking or strengthening your sinful desires?

3. Identify three ways you could sow to the Spirit more in your life.

10

God Recoils in Mercy
(Hosea 11:1-11)

Hosea 11 is one of the most poignant passages in the book. Here we see the broken heart of a doting Father. We get a glimpse of the family photo album: the day of Israel's adoption, their first steps, patching up the grazed knee, lifted up for a kiss. But it is shot through with pain. **The more they were called, the more they went away** (11:2).

1. The Father's tender heart (11:1-4)

> [1]When Israel was a child, I loved him,
>   and out of Egypt I called my son.
> [2]The more they were called,
>   the more they went away;
> they kept sacrificing to the Baals
>   and burning offerings to idols.
> [3]Yet it was I who taught Ephraim to walk;
>   I took them up by their arms,
>   but they did not know that I healed them.
> [4]I led them with cords of kindness,
>   with the bands of love,
> and I became to them as one who eases the yoke on their jaws,
>   and I bent down to them and fed them.

When God commissioned Moses to go to Pharaoh, this is what He told him to say: 'Thus says the LORD, Israel is my firstborn son, and I say to you, "Let my son go that he may serve me." If

179

you refuse to let him go, behold, I will kill your firstborn son' (Exod. 4:22-23). It is the first time in the Bible that God reveals Himself as a Father with Israel as His son. God demands that Pharaoh lets his son go free so that Father and son might be united in worship. If Pharaoh refuses, then Pharaoh's own son will pay the price. And this is indeed what happens with the death of all the firstborn in Egypt – including Pharaoh's own son – in the tenth and final plague.

Hosea 11:1 recalls this event. This was the childhood of the nation when God first chose Israel to be His people, setting His love upon him. When God called Israel out of Egypt, He was calling His son to freedom.

The New Testament sees the exodus from slavery in Egypt as a picture of the work of Jesus. Jesus redeems us from slavery to sin and death through His death, just as God redeemed Israel from slavery in Egypt through the death of the Passover Lamb. But the New Testament also sees this as an act initiated by the Father so that we can know Him as our Father. In Romans 6, Paul reworks the story of the exodus to describe our liberation from sin. In Romans 7, he reworks the giving of the law at Mount Sinai in the light of Christ's coming. Then in Romans 8, he describes how we are led by the Spirit to our glorious inheritance just as Israel was led by the pillars of cloud and fire to their inheritance in the Promised Land. But he also adds:

> For all who are led by the Spirit of God are sons of God. For you did not receive the spirit of slavery to fall back into fear, but you have received the Spirit of adoption as sons, by whom we cry, 'Abba! Father!' The Spirit himself bears witness with our spirit that we are children of God. (Rom. 8:14-16)

Israel discovered her identity as God's son through the exodus. In the same way, Christians discover that we are God's children through our exodus.

The problem was that Israel kept forgetting her new identity. The people did not live as liberated sons, but as vulnerable orphans who needed the protection of other gods. Hosea 11:2 continues: **The more they were called, the more they went away; they kept sacrificing to the Baals and burning offerings to idols.**

We can use our own experience of family life to visualise God's affection for His people and His tenderness towards them. Meditate on His affection and tenderness towards you. Then imagine the pain of betrayal. Imagine the pain God feels at your sin.

Imagine young children running off in a park. Fearing for their safety, their father calls them back. But his shout frightens them. They fear the punishment of the father. And so they run further away. This is how we are to picture Israel. The more God called, the further Israel ran from him. Why? Because they did not trust the grace of God. They did not see themselves as children.

The great English Puritan John Owen wrote: 'So long as the Father is seen as harsh, judging and condemning, the soul is filled with fear and dread every time it comes to him. So in Scripture we read of sinners fleeing and hiding from Him. But when God, who is the Father, is seen as a father, filled with love, the soul is filled with love to God in return.'[1] This is why Hosea 11:3-4 continues:

> Yet it was I who taught Ephraim to walk;
>   I took them up by their arms,
>   but they did not know that I healed them.
> I led them with cords of kindness,
>   with the bands of love,
> and I became to them as one who eases the yoke on their jaws,
>   and I bent down to them and fed them.

The imagery is so tender. We have all seen small children taking their first steps supported by their father or clinging to his hand. This is the image that Hosea evokes to describe God's love for Israel. God is Father who held Israel by the hands as Israel took its first steps.

Then the picture shifts somewhat. Imagine a sick child. Her father forces her to take medicine she hates and refuses her the treats she wants. The child protests at her father's apparently cruel treatment. This is how Israel views God's involvement in her life. But any onlooker can see the father is acting in love

---

1.   John Owen, *Communion with God*, abridged by R. J. K. Law (Banner of Truth, 1991), 18.

for the child's good. **They did not know that I healed them,** says the God of Israel.

The second half of verse 4 is hard to translate. It could be a change of metaphor back to the farming imagery of chapter 10. This is how the ESV understands it. **I led them with cords of kindness ... and I became to them as one who eases the yoke on their jaws.** This is the most natural translation of the word translated 'yoke'. But it involves an awkward switch of metaphor and yokes fall across backs rather than go through jaws. 'Yoke' has the same consonants as the word 'child' and this fits the context better. So it may be better to translate it as the NIV does: **I led them with cords of human kindness, with ties of love. To them I was like one who lifts a little child to the cheek, and I bent down to feed them.** Again, it is a very tender image. First we see God lifting Israel into His arms and nuzzling her into His cheek. Then we see Him bending down to feed her. Again, the importance of this vision of the Father's tender heart is underlined by John Owen:

> Many saints have no greater burden in their lives than that their hearts do not constantly delight and rejoice in God. There is still in them a resistance to walking close with God ... The more we see of God's love, so much more shall we delight in him. All that we learn of God will only frighten us away from him if we do not see him as loving and merciful to us. But if your heart is taken up with the Father's love as the chief property of his nature, it cannot help but choose to be over-powered, conquered and embraced by him. This, if anything, will arouse our desire to make our eternal home with God. If the love of a father will not make a child delight in him, what will? So do this: set your thoughts on the eternal love of the Father and see if your heart is not aroused to delight in him. Sit down for a while at this delightful spring of living water and you will soon find its streams sweet and delightful. You who used to run from God will not now be able, even for a second, to keep at any distance from him.[2]

2. The Father's broken heart (11:5-7)

According to Deuteronomy 21:18-21, the punishment for a persistently rebellious son was death. 'If a man has a stubborn

---

2.   John Owen, *Communion with God*, 32-3.

and rebellious son who will not obey the voice of his father or the voice of his mother ... all the men of the city shall stone him to death with stones.' It sounds harsh to us. But there was an important rationale behind it. Deuteronomy 21:21 continues: 'So you shall purge the evil from your midst, and all Israel shall hear, and fear.' Individual Israelites had to learn parental obedience because Israel itself was the son of God and needed to be an obedient son.

In Deuteronomy 5, Moses reminds the people of the Ten Commandments, including the fifth commandment with its call to 'Honour your father and your mother.' This commandment has a promised attached to it: 'that your days may be long, and that it may go well with you in the land that the LORD your God is giving you' (5:16). Moses echoes these words in his conclusion to his reiteration of the Ten Commandments: 'You shall walk in all the way that the LORD your God has commanded you, that you may live, and that it may go well with you, and that you may live long in the land that you shall possess.' (Deut. 5:33) The fifth commandment does not arbitrarily have a promise attached to it. Israelite children had to learn to be obedient to their parents. In so doing, they were learning a pattern of parental obedience that would shape the culture of the nation. The nation as a whole would become an obedient son of God and they would therefore remain long in the Promised Land. But if Israel becomes a disobedient son, then it will not remain in the land. It will be exiled.

And Israel has been a rebellious son and now God spells its punishment.

> ⁵They shall not return to the land of Egypt,
>   but Assyria shall be their king,
>   because they have refused to return to me.
> ⁶The sword shall rage against their cities,
>   consume the bars of their gates,
>   and devour them because of their own counsels.
> ⁷My people are bent on turning away from me,
>   and though they call out to the Most High,
>   he shall not raise them up at all. (11:5-7)

Verse 5 could be: **They shall not return to the land of Egypt, but Assyria shall be their king** (ESV). In other words, long ago

Israel was enslaved by Egypt, but now they will be enslaved by Assyria. Or verse 5 could be: **Will they not return to Egypt and will not Assyria rule over them?** (NIV). Israel will return to slavery in Egypt, only this time it will be Assyria. In other words, their return to Egypt will be metaphorical. The reality is exile in Assyria. We have met this idea before in Hosea 9:3: 'They shall not remain in the land of the LORD, but Ephraim shall return to Egypt, and they shall eat unclean food in Assyria.' (See also 8:13.) Israel's fate will be *like* a reversal of the exodus story. It will be *like* a return to slavery in Egypt. But it is Assyria who will defeat them and enslave them – not Egypt.

The clause **they call out to the Most High** in verse 7 is literally 'upwards they call on him'. The NIV and ESV take this as a reference to 'God Most High'. But this reading is hard to reconcile with the previous line, where the people are bent on turning away from the LORD. Indeed, the grammar suggests the calling upwards is an elaboration of the previous line. So it is more likely to be a reference to the mountain shrines of Baal. The call upwards is not a call to heaven where the Lord dwells, but to the mountains where the Baals dwell. In other words, their backsliding took the form of calling on Baals instead of calling on God.

Verse 5 begins and ends with the same word: **repent** ('return' and 'repent' in the NIV). Israel will 'return' to Egypt (= Assyria) because they refuse to 'return' to God. In fact, they are determined to 'turn' away from him (11:7).

Matthew quotes these verses in his account of the flight of Jesus into Egypt: '[Joseph] rose and took the child and his mother by night and departed to Egypt and remained there until the death of Herod. This was to fulfil what the Lord had spoken by the prophet, "Out of Egypt I called my son"' (Matt. 2:14-15). Hosea was talking about Israel's past, not the Messiah's future. So at first sight Hosea 11:1 can seem an odd verse for Matthew to apply to Jesus. But Matthew knew that Jesus had done what Israel had failed to do. Jesus is God's faithful and obedient Son. The son that God had originally called out of Egypt had proved disobedient and false. Now in Jesus another Son has come back from exile in Egypt and He proves to be a true Son. When we put our faith in Christ,

He becomes our representative. We are *in* Christ. And it is in Christ that we are treated as God's beloved children – even when we are unfaithful and disobedient.

3. The Father's merciful heart (11:8-9)

These verses take us to the heart of Hosea's message. The Old Testament scholar Gerhard von Rad calls them 'an utterance whose daring is unparalleled in the whole of prophecy'.[3] In verses 1-7, we saw God's tender, fatherly love for His people. But His people have been a rebellious son who deserves judgment. Is there any hope for this family?

> How can I give you up, O Ephraim?
> How can I hand you over, O Israel?
> How can I make you like Admah?
> How can I treat you like Zeboiim?
> My heart recoils within me;
> my compassion grows warm and tender. (11:8)

Here we see the heart of God. The verdict against His people is clear. Judgment is certain. But here we see God's anguish at that thought. Admah and Zeboiim were two of the five cities destroyed along with Sodom and Gomorrah (Gen. 19; see also Deut. 29:23). God cannot bear to think of His people sharing the same fate.

> I will not execute my burning anger;
> I will not again destroy Ephraim;
> for I am God and not a man,
> the Holy One in your midst,
> and I will not come in wrath. (11:9)

I will not again destroy Ephraim is literally 'I will return to ruin Ephraim' or 'I will turn from ruining Ephraim'. In verse 5, Israel refused to 'return' (or repent) to God. So they deserve to 'return' to slavery. But now God 'turns'. He turns away from His anger. It may be an allusion to the story of Sodom and Gomorrah when God sent angels ahead to investigate the evil of the cities before returning to destroy them.

Why will God turn from His anger? Because he is **the Holy One**. That is a surprise! We normally associate God's holiness

---

3.   von Rad, *Old Testament Theology Volume II*, 145.

with His purity and opposition to sin. But God's holiness is His distinctiveness. The word 'holy' means 'set apart'. God is set apart from human beings in that He is different from us. He is not like human beings. Usually in Scripture, His holiness describes the contrast between our sin and God's purity. But here it describes the contrast between our resentments and God's grace. A typical human response to being wronged is revenge. But, says God, **I am God and not a man**. In other words, God's response to the sin of His people is not like human responses. The divine response to being wronged is grace. Commenting on this verse, John Newton wrote:

> If we had offended men, or angels, as we have offended our Creator and Redeemer, and they had permission and power to punish us, our case would be utterly desperate. Only he who made us, is able to bear with us. All the attributes (as we speak) of the infinite God must of course be equally infinite. As is his majesty, so is his mercy.[4]

We too easily think God is angry with His people in the way we are angry with people. We, for example, often give people the cold shoulder until the fault is forgotten. But God is much more serious about sin than this. Sin does not simply fade from His memory. He does not get in a bad mood that gradually dissipates. His anger is His consistent hatred of sin.

But God is also much more serious about love than this. His love is not changeable. It does not depend on how we treat Him. He is committed to His people and determined to show them mercy. The phrase **I am God and not a man** echoes Numbers 23:19: 'God is not man, that he should lie, or a son of man, that he should change his mind. Has he said, and will he not do it? Or has he spoken, and will he not fulfil it?' It suggests God is making a covenant oath. We can be sure He will do what He says because God always does what He says He will do. He commits Himself to mercy.

So how can God be determined to judge in verses 5-7 and then be determined to save in verses 8-9? God's determination to judge and His determination to save sit uncomfortably beside one another in Hosea, almost as if God cannot make

---

4.   John Newton, 'Motives to Humiliation and Praise', *Works*, Banner of Truth, 1820, 1985, Volume 2, 296-7.

up His mind. But they are resolved at the cross. At the cross, God's determination to judge and His determination to save are both realised. His judgment does not compromise His mercy and His mercy does not compromise His judgment. This is how Paul explains it in Romans 3:23-26:

> For all have sinned and fall short of the glory of God, and are justified by his grace as a gift, through the redemption that is in Christ Jesus, whom God put forward as a propitiation by his blood, to be received by faith. This was to show God's righteousness, because in his divine forbearance he had passed over former sins. It was to show his righteousness at the present time, so that he might be just and the justifier of the one who has faith in Jesus.

The word 'propitiation' means 'turning aside wrath'. At the cross, God turned aside His wrath from us and directed it towards Jesus in our place. As a result, God both justly judges and graciously saves. God does not condemn His rebellious children because the Father and Son agreed together that the Father would condemn His own Son in our place. 'In this is love, not that we have loved God but that he loved us and sent his Son to be the propitiation for our sins' (1 John 4:10).

Above we quoted from Deuteronomy 21 describing the death penalty that should fall on a disobedient son. It is the same passage that says: 'And if a man has committed a crime punishable by death and he is put to death, and you hang him on a tree, his body shall not remain all night on the tree, but you shall bury him the same day, for a hanged man is cursed by God' (21:22-23). Galatians 3:13 uses this verse to describe the cross of Jesus. Jesus dies the death of a disobedient son under the curse of God. He Himself was the true and obedient Son. But He dies in the place of disobedient children so we can share His sonship.

In Genesis 19, the word that is used to describe God's judgment on the cities of Admah and Zeboiim is 'overthrow'. We are told 'he overthrew those cities, and all the valley, and all the inhabitants of the cities, and what grew on the ground' (Gen. 19:25). The same word is used in Deuteronomy 29. Moses describes the curses that will fall on Israel if they are unfaithful to God. 'The whole land burned out with brimstone and salt, nothing sown and nothing growing, where no plant can sprout, an overthrow like that of Sodom and Gomorrah, Admah, and Zeboiim, which the LORD overthrew in his anger and wrath' (Deut. 29:23). Admah and Zeboiim, along with Sodom and Gomorrah, have become a paradigm for God's judgment. This is what God's judgment looks like. It looks like 'overthrow'.

The same word **overthrow** is used in verse 8. The NIV translates it 'changed' (**My heart is changed within me**) and the ESV translates it as **recoils** (**My heart recoils within me**). The link is clearest in the NASB: **My heart is turned over within me**. At Admah and Zeboiim, there was an overthrow. And now again there is an overthrow. But this time the overthrow is within God Himself. This time it is God who is overthrown. The judgment that fell on Sodom and Gomorrah, and Admah and Zeboiim, falls again. But this time it falls on God Himself in the person of His Son.

How can I make you like Admah? How can I treat you like Zeboiim?, God asks. The answer is that He does not treat us like Admah and Zeboiim because His Son was treated like them in our place.

4. The Father's missional heart (11:10-11)

In verses 10-11, Hosea introduces a new metaphor. We hear the Lion roar:

> ¹⁰They shall go after the LORD;
>   he will roar like a lion;
> when he roars,
>   his children shall come trembling from the west;
> ¹¹they shall come trembling like birds from Egypt,
>   and like doves from the land of Assyria,
>   and I will return them to their homes, declares the LORD.

God not only forgives our sin. His roar will summon His children back to the land. He will restore us to a relationship with Him. This was partly fulfilled when the southern tribes returned from exile in Babylon. It was partly fulfilled in the book of Acts as the gospel went from Jerusalem to Samaria (where the remnant of the northern tribes lived). It is being fulfilled as God's children around the world are summoned by His roar. Whenever we proclaim the gospel, the Lion roars. Let that thought sink in for a moment. When you tell your neighbour or colleague about Jesus, the Lion is roaring. The faltering words that stumble out of our mouths are the roar of the Lion. Like Aslan in the Chronicles of Narnia by C. S. Lewis, it is a roar that makes people tremble. But it is also a roar that leads people home.

In verse 1, God called His people **out of Egypt**. Now they will again come from Egypt. There is going to be a second exodus. The first exodus under Moses was a real liberation of people from slavery. But it was also a picture of salvation. It pointed forward to the work of Christ. Jesus is the true Passover Lamb who liberates us from the ultimate tyranny of sin and death.

STUDY QUESTIONS

1. In what ways does your experience of family life help you understand God's relationship with His people?

2. How is divine anger different from most human anger?

3. How can God be both determined to judge and determined to save?

4. How does God the Lion roar today?

5. What happens when God the Lion roars today?

6. How has Hosea 11 revised or renewed your view of God?

7. How has Hosea 11 revised or renewed your view of mission?

Questions for Personal Reflection

1. How has your experience of your father positively or negatively shaped your understanding of God as Father?

2. Do you run from God or do you run to God? What about when you sin?

3. Reread the quotations from John Owen. Pray through these quotations, applying them to your relationship with God the Father.

11

God Revisits Our History
(Hosea 11:12–13:16)

How is your life going? How is your business? How is your work? Or how is your school life? I suspect that some readers will be upbeat about life. Business is booming. Work is rewarding. You are getting good grades at school. The sun is shining. Life is good. Others will be facing problems. Business is tough. Clients are hard to find. Or work is a struggle. Perhaps talk of redundancy is in the air. Or exams are looming and you are worried about how you will do.

I guess most of us could put ourselves in one of those two categories, triumph or disaster. Or at least put different parts of our lives in those categories. Rudyard Kipling famously wrote, 'If you can meet with Triumph and Disaster, and treat those two impostors just the same ... you'll be a Man, my son!'

Chapters 12 and 13 of Hosea equip us to face the triumphs and disasters of life. And they do so by teaching us some lessons from history. Hosea looks at three key periods from Israel's past.

1. The lesson of Jacob: We are who we are by God's grace (11:12–12:6)

It is not our triumphs and disasters that make us who we are. Ultimately, it is not our triumphs and disasters that define us. Instead it is God's grace.

Hosea takes us back to the story of Jacob. Abraham was the great founding father of God's people. His son Isaac had twins, Esau and Jacob. God gave Jacob a new name, Israel. Jacob was rarely called 'Israel' during his lifetime. But it became the name by which his descendants were known, the nation of Israel. Hosea is playing on this. The story of Israel the nation parallels the story of Israel the person. What was that story?

Hosea begins in the womb, where Jacob grabbed hold of Esau's heel so that they came out together. Genesis 25:22-26 says:

> The children struggled together within her, and she said, 'If it is thus, why is this happening to me?' So she went to enquire of the LORD. And the LORD said to her, 'Two nations are in your womb, and two peoples from within you shall be divided; the one shall be stronger than the other, the older shall serve the younger.' When her days to give birth were completed, behold, there were twins in her womb. The first came out red, all his body like a hairy cloak, so they called his name Esau. Afterwards his brother came out with his hand holding Esau's heel, so his name was called Jacob.

Hosea recounts this episode: **In the womb he took his brother by the heel** (12:3). 'Jacob' means 'he grasps'. Jacob was a 'grasper'. If someone is ruthless in their pursuit of money or advancement, then we say they are 'grasping'. So it was with Jacob. What happened to him in the womb also set the pattern of his life.

But 'Jacob' also became an idiom for deceit. Jacob is a 'deceiver'. That is because when Isaac came towards the end of his life he had to pass on the inheritance and bless his elder son, who, of course, was Esau and not Jacob. In Genesis 27, we read how Isaac told Esau to hunt wild game and prepare a meal during which Isaac would bless him. But Isaac's wife Rebekah overheard this and came up with a plan to deceive her husband. While Esau is out hunting, she got Jacob to kill two domestic goats. She then prepared the meal while Jacob dressed in Esau's clothes and wrapped animal skin around his arms so he smelt and felt like Esau who was naturally hairy. Isaac said, 'The voice is Jacob's voice, but the hands are the hands of Esau' (Gen. 27:22). 'Are you really my son, Esau?' he asked (Gen. 27:24). And Jacob answered 'I am.' So Isaac blessed Jacob and the promise of God passed to Jacob. God's people came from Jacob's line. The promised Messiah came from Jacob's line and not from Esau's. All this because Jacob was a deceiver. Israel the person was a deceiver.

Now look at 11:12-12:1:

> ¹²Ephraim has surrounded me with lies,
>   and the house of Israel with deceit,
> but Judah still walks with God
>   and is faithful to the Holy One.
> ^{12:1}Ephraim feeds on the wind
>   and pursues the east wind all day long;
> they multiply falsehood and violence;
>   they make a covenant with Assyria,
>   and oil is carried to Egypt.

These verses tell us that Israel the nation also was a deceiver. They had made a covenant with God. They swore promises to Him. But now they are off, making treaties with Assyria and Egypt. The oil being carried down to Egypt is tribute to seal the deal. The flimsy and elusive nature of these commitments is emphasised with the image of Ephraim (another name for Israel) feeding on the wind and chasing it. Perhaps the idea is the futility of trying to herd the wind. A meal of wind is never going to nourish, and no amount of pursuit can bring the east wind under our control. Similarly, Egypt and Assyria cannot nourish the needs of Israel, nor will they be bent to Israel's purposes. A contract with the wind would provide about as much security as a covenant with Egypt or Assyria could provide.

The reference to Judah is ambiguous as the contrasting translations of the ESV and NIV reveal: **Judah still walks with God and is faithful to the Holy One** (ESV), as opposed to **Judah is unruly against God, even against the faithful Holy One** (NIV). This may well be a deliberate ambiguity. Hosea does not use 'Yahweh' or 'the LORD' – God's covenant name. Instead, he uses the generic term for 'God/god'. Judah is faithful to a deity, but is it the LORD? Israel is deceitful. Is Judah any better? It is for Hosea's Judean readers to decide.

Is deceit the way forward? The image of the wind suggests not. But what lessons do we learn from history? Does Jacob triumph over Esau because he is deceitful? Does he become a great nation because he is grasping? Is that the lesson we should learn?

Come back to the story of Israel the person. Esau, as you can imagine, is not best pleased with what Jacob had done. So Jacob has to flee for his life. At this point, he has nothing except God's promise. On the run from Esau, he collapses at night and begs God for help. And God comes to him and speaks to him. He gives him a vision of heaven opened, a sign of His grace. And Jacob calls that place 'Bethel' (Gen. 28:19). **He met God at Bethel**, says Hosea, **and there God spoke with us – the LORD, the God of hosts, the LORD is his memorial name'** (12:4-5).

Years later, Jacob is still on the run and has nowhere to go but back home (Gen. 31). And so he prepares to meet Esau again, not knowing how Esau will react. The night before he expects to meet Esau, he is alone. God comes to him in the form of an angel (Gen. 32:22-32). And Jacob wrestles with the angel. They wrestle all night until, as dawn is breaking, Jacob overcomes the angel and wrestles a blessing from God. This is the moment when God gives him the name 'Israel' which means 'fights with God'. Hosea recalls this story in verse 3-4: **In the womb he took his brother by the heel, and in his manhood he strove with God. He strove with the angel and prevailed; he wept and sought his favour.**

God's people are like their ancestor. They are deceiving and grasping. The LORD has a charge against them, just as He had against Jacob (and just as He did in 4:1). **The LORD has an indictment against Judah and will punish Jacob according to his ways; he will repay him according to his deeds** (12:2). Jacob lived a life of deceit and grasping. And so God comes against Jacob with this indictment. But Jacob wrestled with God *and sought His grace*. Verse 4 says: **He wept and sought his favour**.

So Hosea is saying to his hearers/readers, 'You are like your father Jacob. You are full of deceit. You are constantly grasping. So God has a charge against you. But learn the lesson of history. Jacob became Israel not through his grasping and deceit, but because he sought God's grace. It was not his grasping that made him who he was. It was God's grace.'

Kipling was right. Triumph and Disaster are impostors in this sense: they do not make us who we are. They do not define us. We are who we are by God's grace.

At the two crisis moments of his life, Jacob sought God and found God. He sought God and heard God. Look again at 12:4-5:

> ⁴He strove with the angel and prevailed;
>   he wept and sought his favour.
> He met God at Bethel,
>   and there God spoke with us –
> ⁵the LORD, the God of hosts,
>   the LORD is his memorial name:

Jacob fought for God's grace. But how can we fight for grace? Surely it is not grace if we have to wrestle it from God? Grace is God blessing us *as a gift* – for no good reason other than His love. You cannot *earn* grace or *win* grace – if you could, it would not be grace! So how can we fight for grace? For that matter, how does Jacob defeat God in a wrestling match? For that is what Hosea says in 12:4: Jacob **overcame** God. The best answer I can give is this:

1. *God makes Himself weak so He can bless us.* That is what He does with Jacob. He lets Himself be defeated by Jacob so that He can bless Jacob. And that is what He does at the cross. He lets Himself be defeated by humanity so that He can bless us.

2. *God makes us strong so He can bless us.* Verse 6 is literally **return *with* our God**. The ESV translates it: **So you, by the help of your God, return, hold fast to love and justice, and wait continually for your God.** God Himself empowers us to fight Him for His grace. It is a battle He wants us to win. We fight *for* grace *through* grace.

The idea of wrestling with God captures the urgency, the passion, the fervour of our need of grace and desire for grace and love for grace. We are to be people who fervently seek God's grace and who are passionate about His grace.

But we do so in God's power. God fought against Jacob, but He also empowered Jacob's victory! Our longing for God is evidence of God's work in us. Our seeking after God is proof of God's work in us.

That is often the dynamic of our relationship with God. I have written a lot about passion as we have looked at the message of Hosea. But what do you do when you do not feel passionate? What do you do when you feel a bit flat? Or maybe you acknowledge that the truths of the gospel are amazing, but they just do not feel amazing? What do you do?

The answer is, You fight! You fight for God's blessing. You fight for His favour. Pray until God moves you. Search His Word until it blesses you. Think of yourself as wrestling in prayer for God's blessing. But know this: When you wrestle with God and win His blessing God has not only fought *against* you, He has also fought *for* you. He has empowered your longing. Why? Because He wants a relationship with you. He wants you to pursue Him, to long for, to seek Him and in this seeking to find Him and know Him and love Him.

Learn the lesson of history: We are who we are by God's grace. That is not the message of our culture. Our culture says, 'You can take hold of your identity. You can make yourself the person you want to be. Work hard. Pass your exams. Make it in business. Climb the career ladder. Grasp. Look after number one.'

Verse 3 informs us: **In the womb he took his brother by the heel, and in his manhood he strove with God.** Hosea's message is this: Be a grasping person. But do not be like the young Jacob, grasping at people. Be like the old Jacob, grasping at God. Seek God. Wait for God. Struggle with God. Beg God for His grace.

2. The lesson of Moses: We have what we have by God's grace (12:7–13:8)

According to 12:8, Ephraim says, **Ah, but I am rich; I have found wealth for myself.** Ephraim is another name for Israel. Israel boasts in her wealth. **I have found wealth *for myself*.** In 12:6, Hosea's call is to return with God's help. But Israel's boast is: 'I've earned it. I don't need God's help.' It was the same temptation that the church in Laodicea would face over 700 years later. In Revelation 3:17, the risen Lord says to them: 'For you say, I am rich, I have prospered, and I need nothing, not realising that you are wretched, pitiable, poor, blind, and naked.' This attitude continues to be prevalent among middle-class people in the Western world. 'I have what I have through my achievements,' people say. 'I am a self-made man.' 'I don't need God.'

So Hosea refers to the next period in the story. Israel the man went to Egypt to escape famine. And there in Egypt, over a 400-year period, Israel the man became Israel the nation. But there in Egypt the nation was enslaved. God, however, heard their cries (Exod. 2:23-25). He called Moses to lead His people out of Egypt. He revealed His name to Moses as the LORD, Yahweh, the covenant God of Israel. He rescued His people out of Egypt. He provided for them as He led them through the wilderness. He brought them to the land He had promised to Abraham. It was inhabited by the Canaanites, but God defeated the Canaanites and gave His people the land as a gift, a land flowing with milk and honey. Hosea recalls this story in 12:9: **I have been the LORD your God ever since you came out of Egypt** (NIV). 'I revealed myself to you as the LORD and have been your covenant God ever since.'

Hosea continues the story in 12:12-13: **Jacob fled to the land of Aram; there Israel served for a wife, and for a wife he guarded sheep. By a prophet the Lord brought Israel up from Egypt, and by a prophet he was guarded.** Here is another episode from the story of Jacob. When Jacob fled from Esau, he went to live with his uncle Laban. There he fell in love with Laban's daughter Rachel. Genesis 29 tells the story of how Jacob spent seven years tending sheep for Laban, earning a dowry to win Rachel. In fact, Laban tricked Jacob and married him to an elder daughter Leah. So Jacob worked a further seven years to earn the right to marry Rachel.

It looks like Hosea has got the chronology wrong. Having told the story of how God rescued Israel from slavery in Egypt, it seems he is slipping back in time. The key thing, however, is the word **guarded**, which appears in both verses 12 and 13. Jacob guarded sheep. In the same way, God sent a prophet, Moses, to **guard** His people. The story of Jacob is recalled to highlight the way that Moses shepherded God's people. The focus is not on Jacob, but on Moses. Here God's people are not like Jacob, but like his sheep! But God cared for them and provided for them through Moses. They have what they have through God's care and provision.

Moses himself is not named in these verses. He is simply described as 'a prophet'. Perhaps the point is to put the focus on God Himself and His Word. The One who shepherded God's people was not so much Moses as God Himself through the words of Moses. This resonates with an intriguing change of pronoun back in 12:4. Hosea says: **He [Jacob] met God at Bethel**. And we might expect him to then say, 'and there God spoke with *him*.' But in fact Hosea says: **and there God spoke with *us***. In others words, the word spoken to Jacob is still spoken to us. Bethel was the place where Jacob met God. And we too can meet with God through His Word. The Bible is our Bethel, the place where we meet God. The Sunday sermon in your church is a Bethel, a place where you can meet God as His Word is expounded. Above all, Jesus is our Bethel. He is the Word of God in whom we meet God. It is by this word that we are fed and guarded, just as Moses fed and guarded the people in his day.

But Israel had aroused God's anger. **Ephraim has given bitter provocation; so his Lord will leave his bloodguilt on him and will repay him for his disgraceful deeds** (12:14). God's people are guilty of Baal worship (13:1). They go from bad to worse: **And now they sin more and more, and make for themselves metal images, idols skilfully made of their silver, all of them the work of craftsmen** (13:2). They even offer human sacrifices: **It is said of them, "Those who offer human sacrifice kiss calves!"** (13:2).

Here is the worst of it. The word **merchant** in 12:7 is literally 'Canaanite': 'The *Canaanite* uses dishonest scales and loves to defraud.' God chose His people to be a light to the nations. He cast the Canaanite nations out of the Promised Land so that there might be a place on earth in which the goodness of His reign could be on display. But now His people are 'Canaanites' (12:7) – 'pagans' we might say. They are no different from the world around them.

And so God says, **I will again make you dwell in tents** (12:9). He will do to His people what He did to the Canaanites: He will cast them out of the land. As we saw in Hosea 9, the story is going to go into reverse! God led His people from tents into the Promised Land. But now he will cast them out of the Promised Land and back into tents.

They will be fleeting and fragile: **Therefore they shall be like the morning mist or like the dew that goes early away, like the chaff that swirls from the threshing floor or like smoke from a window** (13:3). Back in 6:4 God said *their love* was like morning mist. Now, as a result, *they themselves* will be like morning mist (13:3). In other words, they will soon vanish. God is going to be like a lion or a leopard or a bear, ripping them open and devouring them, as 13:7-8 says:

> [7]So I am to them like a lion;
>   like a leopard I will lurk beside the way.
> [8]I will fall upon them like a bear robbed of her cubs;
>   I will tear open their breast,
> and there I will devour them like a lion,
>   as a wild beast would rip them open.

What is the lesson of history? We have what we have by God's grace. 13:4-6 say:

> [4]But I am the LORD your God
>   from the land of Egypt;
> you know no God but me,
>   and besides me there is no saviour.
> [5]It was I who knew you in the wilderness,
>   in the land of drought;
> [6]but when they had grazed, they became full,
>   they were filled, and their heart was lifted up;
>   therefore they forgot me.

The NIV translates verse 6: **When I fed them, they were satisfied; when they were satisfied, they became proud; then they forgot me**. It is a haunting chain of events. It starts with God feeding His people and ends just three steps later with them forgetting Him.

We so often draw the wrong lessons from history. We see our prosperity and triumphs. And we conclude that we are good people or clever people or hard-working people who have earned our reward. Our prosperity leads to self-confidence and self-reliance (12:8; 13:5-6), when all the time it should lead to heartfelt thanks towards God. Our genes, our upbringing, our education, our character, our very breath all come from God.

My job title, my beautiful home, my children's success, my church's success. We all readily claim credit for these. How many times have you prayed for something – for a job interview, an exam, a work project, an evangelistic event. And then when it was successful, attributed that success not to answered prayer, but to your effort or skill?

Our culture says: 'I have what I have through my effort – I am a self-made man.' Our culture says, 'I can spend what I have because I earned it. It's my home, I can do with it what I like.' But God says: **I cared for you ... I fed you** (13:5-6, NIV). **I have been the LORD your God ever since you came out of Egypt** (13:4, NIV). The reality is not 'I can spend what I have because I earned it,' but 'I owe to God what I have because God gave it to me.' Hosea 13:4 tells us: **You shall acknowledge no God but me, no Saviour except me** (NIV).

3. The lesson of King Saul: We will be what we will be by God's grace (13:9-16)

When the nation of Israel first lived in the land, they were ruled over by God Himself. But eventually they asked for a king like the nations. They rejected God's kingship in favour of human kingship. They wanted someone they could see who would rescue them and protect them. And so God gave them a king, Saul

But here is the problem. Human kings are a disappointment. Saul's reign ended in failure. A human king cannot protect you. And, especially, a human king cannot protect you when *your enemy is God Himself*. In 13:9-11 Hosea continues the history lesson:

> [9]He destroys you, O Israel,
>> for you are against me, against your helper.
> [10]Where now is your king, to save you in all your cities?
>> Where are all your rulers –
> those of whom you said,
>> 'Give me a king and princes'?
> [11]I gave you a king in my anger,
>> and I took him away in my wrath.

What use is a human king when you are up against God?
None! There is no help, except in God Himself.

> [12]The iniquity of Ephraim is bound up;
>   his sin is kept in store.
> [13]The pangs of childbirth come for him,
>   but he is an unwise son,
> for at the right time he does not present himself
>   at the opening of the womb.

Much of Hosea's ministry was conducted during good days.
The economy was booming and the nation enjoyed peace. It
was all too easy to draw the conclusion that sin did not matter.
People who sinned seemed to prosper just as much as the
righteous, often more, often at the expense of the righteous.
But Hosea has an explanation. Their sin is being stored up. It
is not that God has failed to notice what is happening, or that
He is indifferent. Paul makes the same point in Romans 2:4-5.
The delay of God's judgment is not a sign of His neglect, but of
'the riches of his kindness and forbearance and patience'. He
is giving humanity an opportunity to repent. 'God's kindness
is meant to lead you to repentance.' 'But because of your hard
and impenitent heart you are storing up wrath for yourself
on the day of wrath when God's righteous judgment will be
revealed.' In the Bible 'the pangs of childbirth' are often used
as a picture of suffering before the coming of God (Rom. 8:22).
Hosea uses it in this way, but it is clear that for his hearers
the coming of God will mean the coming of judgment. They
should read the signs of the times and ready themselves for
the coming judgment by repenting of their sin.

Yet God is the deliverer who defeats our enemies – even
our last and greatest enemy, death. God is our true king, our
true protector, our true redeemer. 13:14 says:

> Shall I ransom them from the power of Sheol?
>   Shall I redeem them from Death?
> O Death, where are your plagues?
>   O Sheol, where is your sting?

This is Hosea's final lesson from history: We will be what
we will be by God's grace. As with the previous lessons, our
culture does not say this. Our culture says, 'I can secure my

future – if I work hard enough or I save hard enough or if I invest or I insure.' People go off to university to secure their future. Every day people go to work to secure a future for them and their children. People pour themselves into their businesses to secure its future. At the weekends they do DIY to maintain a home for the future. Triumph and disaster matter so much to us because we think they define our future. But the reality is we cannot secure our future, certainly not against death.

Let me ask you a question: What is it that gives you confidence for the future? Think about your answer. Does it suggest that you think you are what you are or have what you have or will be what you will be through your effort and achievement? Or are you trusting in God's grace?

Only God can secure our future. Paul quotes Hosea 13:14 in 1 Corinthians 15:54-58:

> When the perishable puts on the imperishable, and the mortal puts on immortality, then shall come to pass the saying that is written:
> 'Death is swallowed up in victory.'
> 'O death, where is your victory?
>   O death, where is your sting?'
> The sting of death is sin, and the power of sin is the law. But thanks be to God, who gives us the victory through our Lord Jesus Christ. Therefore, my beloved brothers, be steadfast, immovable, always abounding in the work of the Lord, knowing that in the Lord your labour is not in vain.

Paul provides a little commentary on this verse from Hosea by answering the questions it poses. They are rhetorical questions in which the answer is clearly 'nowhere'. Where is death's victory and sting? Nowhere. Death has no victory and it has no sting. But Paul drives the point home by answering the rhetorical questions. What is the sting of death? It is sin, Paul says. This is perhaps a bit of surprise. We might suppose that death is the sting of sin. If you indulge in sin then it will sting you with death. Sin leads to death. But Paul says sin is the sting of death. The point is that there is something worse than physical death and that is spiritual death – eternal separation from God in hell. Christians and non-Christians alike experience physical death. But the sting of physical death is the judgment that will follow it on account of sin.

However, for Christians their sin has been dealt with. 'Christ died for our sins,' Paul says at the beginning of the chapter (15:3). Hosea talks about 'bloodguilt': **Ephraim has given bitter provocation; so his Lord will leave his bloodguilt on him and will repay him for his disgraceful deeds** (12:14). **Samaria shall bear her guilt, because she has rebelled against her God** (13:16). But our guilt has been atoned for through the blood of Jesus. God promises in 13:14, **I will redeem them from death** (NIV). So death is disarmed. And where is the victory of death? 'Look, there it is,' says Paul, 'being handed over to us': God 'gives us the victory through our Lord Jesus Christ' (1 Cor. 15:57).

Conclusion

This would be a great moment to end. But this is not the ending. Or at least it is not the only ending. There are two endings to the story. The first ending is this: Death is defeated and victory is ours through Jesus. But the second ending is Hosea 13:14e-16:

> [14]Compassion is hidden from my eyes.
> [15]Though he may flourish among his brothers,
>   the east wind, the wind of the LORD, shall come,
>   rising from the wilderness,
> and his fountain shall dry up;
>   his spring shall be parched;
> it shall strip his treasury
>   of every precious thing.
> [16]Samaria shall bear her guilt,
>   because she has rebelled against her God;
> they shall fall by the sword;
>   their little ones shall be dashed in pieces,
>   and their pregnant women ripped open.

It is horrible! Some of Israel heard Hosea's message, returned to God and were saved. But the nation as a whole ignored him. The Assyrian army came, besieged the capital Samaria and crushed the people, wiping them from history. Their story came to an end. Israel appeared to thrive. **He may flourish among his brothers**, says Hosea in verse 15. It looks successful. It triumphs. But it misunderstood its triumph. And, as a result, God's judgment was just over the horizon. An east wind would come, bringing disaster. Her fertility would be gone, her storehouses plundered, her people dashed to the ground. Samaria must bear her guilt. And so it will be for all who do not return to God. So Hosea's message comes to us:

> You must return to your God;
>> maintain love and justice,
>> and wait for your God always ...
> I will deliver this people from the power of the grave;
>> I will redeem them from death. (12:6; 13:14, NIV)

STUDY QUESTIONS

1. What lessons do we learn from the story of Jacob? Which are particularly pertinent to your situation?

2. What does it mean to wrestle with God?

3. How do these chapters speak to a culture that is grasping?

4. How do these chapters speak to a culture that prides itself on its self-reliance?

5. How do these chapters speak to a culture that is trying to create a secure future?

Questions for Personal Reflection

1. To what do you attribute your successes?

2. Review the ways that God has been involved in your successes.

3. What gives you confidence for the future? Your answer will reveal what your faith is in.

12

God Welcomes Us Home
(Hosea 14:1-9)

Hosea tells the story of Israel's unfaithfulness, and not only her unfaithfulness but also that of all humanity. We are all like an adulterous bride who turns away from God's love to other lovers who use and abuse her.

So Hosea tells the story of God's judgment against Israel, and not only Israel but all humanity. God is against us. We have provoked His jealous anger. Hosea warned that God would come against Israel. And this is what happened. The Assyrian army defeated and destroyed the northern tribes, wiping them from the map. And God is coming against us in an even more terrible judgment.

But Hosea also tells the story of God's continuing love for His people. The distinctive message of Hosea is this sense of God's passion for them.

> 'I am now going to allure her;
>   I will lead her into the wilderness and speak tenderly to
> her ...'
> 'In that day,' declares the LORD, 'you will call me "my hus-
> band";
>   you will no longer call me "my master" ...'
> 'I will betroth you to me for ever;
>   I will betroth you in righteousness and justice,
>   in love and compassion.' (2:14, 16, 19)

We see the heart of God exposed, raw and wounded, tender and passionate:

> When Israel was a child, I loved him,
>> and out of Egypt I called my son.
> But the more they were called,
>> the more they went away from me ...
> It was I who taught Ephraim to walk,
>> taking them by the arms;
> but they did not realise
>> it was I who healed them.
> I led them with cords of human kindness,
>> with ties of love.
> To them I was like one who lifts
>> a little child to the cheek,
>> and I bent down to feed them ...
> How can I give you up, Ephraim?
>> How can I hand you over, Israel? ...
> My heart is changed within me;
>> all my compassion is aroused. (11:1-4, 8 NIV)

And so we come to chapter 14. It is a wonderful climax to the message of Hosea. It provides us with a prayer of repentance and a song full of promise, a song that God Himself sings to win our hearts. If chapter 2 told us that God was going to woo us, then here is God's love song. But first we must come home.

Our liturgy of turning (14:1-3)

> [1]Return, O Israel, to the LORD your God,
>> for you have stumbled because of your iniquity.
> [2]Take with you words
>> and return to the LORD;
> say to him,
>> 'Take away all iniquity;
> accept what is good,
>> and we will pay with bulls
>> the vows of our lips.
> [3]Assyria shall not save us;
>> we will not ride on horses;
> and we will say no more, "Our God",
>> to the work of our hands.
> In you the orphan finds mercy.'

This is our liturgy of turning. The word **return** in verse 1 and 2 is literally 'turn'. Hosea is informing us how we can turn back to God. This chapter shows us the way home to God. If you feel far from God, then this chapter is for you. Maybe you are a Christian who feels dry and you have lost your intimacy with God. Or maybe you have never known God. At best He has been an idea, but you have never known Him as a Father. Hosea is showing us the way home to God.

What does Hosea say? **Take with you words** (14:2). Say something to God. Speak. Maybe you have never prayed before. Maybe the whole idea just feels weird. But give it a go. If the prophet Hosea were here now, he would say, 'Speak to God. Take words with you.' What are you going to say? Hosea suggests three things.

1. Ask God for forgiveness (14:2)

'Say to him: Forgive all our sins and receive us graciously, that we may offer the fruit of our lips (NIV). We begin with a prayer of confession and repentance.

Receive us graciously is literally 'accept what is good' (ESV). And **that we may offer the fruit of our lips** is literally 'so that we may pay bulls, our lips'. It could be 'we will pay our vows with (sacrificial) bulls' or 'we will offer our words like (sacrificial) bulls' or (following the Septuagint, the Greek version of the Old Testament) 'we will give you the fruit of our lips.' I think what it means is 'we will offer our words like (sacrificial) bulls.' Our words will be like sacrifices offered on the altar before God. It harks back to something God has previously said through Hosea: 'For I desire steadfast love and not sacrifice, the knowledge of God rather than burnt offerings' (6:6). Or when King David had sinned against God, he said:

> O Lord, open my lips,
> and my mouth will declare your praise.
> For you will not delight in sacrifice, or I would give it;
> you will not be pleased with a burnt offering.
> The sacrifices of God are a broken spirit;
> a broken and contrite heart, O God, you will not despise.
> (Ps. 51:15-17)

In other words, God does not want you to be religious. He does not want you to sort your life out before you come to Him. He does not want some grand gesture. He wants your heart. He wants a broken and contrite heart. This is the good thing that He accepts: a heart that acknowledges your unfaithfulness and comes to Him for forgiveness. 'O Lord, open my lips,' said David. **Take with you words**, says Hosea. Say something. Say that you are sorry.

2. Renounce false security (14:3)

Hosea continues: **Assyria shall not save us; we will not ride on horses; and we will say no more, "Our God", to the work of our hands**.

Assyria was the regional superpower at that time. So it was tempting for Israel to think that an alliance with Assyria would save them. But the irony was that Assyria would be the nation that destroyed Israel. **Horses** were a symbol of military power. They were the equivalent of arming yourself, packing a piece or having a massive army (Ps. 20:7-8). So this is a repudiation of all false gods and false hopes.

Not many of us are tempted to turn to Assyria. Nor will most readers have a horse and if you do I doubt you rely on it for your future! But let me ask you this: How would you complete this sentence? 'I will really be happy when …' Or what about this sentence? 'My future will be secure if …' Is God at the heart of how you completed those sentences? Or did you say, 'When I get married … when I get a job … when I buy a house … when I get an iPad … when I save enough to retire … if I pass my exams … if I get promotion.' In what are you putting your hope?

In Hosea 13, we saw that nothing can protect us from the last enemy, which is death. Nothing – except God who has redeemed us from the grave and disarmed death (13:14). And what we will see in a moment is that nothing can truly satisfy, truly make us flourish, apart from God. So turn from false hopes.

Remember that Hosea has invited us to 'take with you words'. He says, **We will *say* no more, "Our God", to the work of our hands**. This is an invitation not merely to repent, but to renounce. It is an invitation not merely to *think* about turning from false security, but to *say* that that we are turning from false security.

We turn *from* false security and instead turn *to* the compassionate arms of God. This is the third thing that Hosea tells us to say to God: to express our faith in His fatherly love.

3. *Express your faith in God's fatherly love*

Verse 3 concludes: **In you the orphan finds mercy.** In Hosea, we have already met a fatherless child who finds compassion. Back in chapter 1, Hosea has three children. When Hosea's second child is born, God says, 'Call her name No Mercy, for I will no more have mercy on the house of Israel, to forgive them at all' (1:6). And when Hosea's third child is born, God says, 'Call his name Not My People, for you are not my people, and I am not your God' (1:9). The names of those poor children represent Israel and indeed all humanity. We were born to be God's children. But we have turned from God's love and have become fatherless children without His love. That may be who you are: a child without a heavenly Father. If you are, you have made yourself a spiritual orphan. You have walked away from a Father's love. You are orphaned by God's judgment.

But God is the God in whom the fatherless find compassion. At the beginning of his message, Hosea says: 'In the place where it was said to them, "You are not my people," it shall be said to them, "Children of the living God" ... Say to your brothers, "You are my people," and to your sisters, "You have received mercy"' (1:10; 2:1). So, brothers, let me tell you this: 'In Christ we are the people of God. Though we were fatherless, we have become the sons of God. Brothers, we are sons of the living God.' And, sisters, let me tell you this: 'Jesus says to you, "My loved one". Though you have lived without God's love, God says to you now, "My loved one."'

So turn. Take words with you. Come and say to Him, 'In you the fatherless find compassion. Forgive all my sin. I turn from all my other hopes and put my hope in your compassion. Love like me like a father.'

God's song of turning (14:4-8)

What will God's response be? God responds with a song of *His* turning. Verse 4 says: **I will heal their apostasy; I will love them freely, for my anger has turned from them**. The word **apostasy** is another word for 'turning'. God says, 'I will heal their turning – their turning away – and love them freely.'

But then God says – and this is the astonishing twist of chapter 14 – **for my anger has turned from them**. It is the same word again: 'turn'. Verse 1 says *Return*, **O Israel, to the LORD your God** and verse 2 says **Take with you words and** *return* **to the LORD**. Israel must turn back to God. But now it is God who turns! God Himself turns. He turns His anger away. This is what he said in 11:8-9:

> How can I give you up, O Ephraim?
> > How can I hand you over, O Israel? ...
> My heart recoils within me;
> > my compassion grows warm and tender.
> I will not execute my burning anger,
> > I will not again destroy Ephraim;
> for I am God, and not a man,
> > the Holy One in your midst.

'I will not again destroy Ephraim' is literally 'I will *turn* from ruining Ephraim'. God has turned His righteous anger away from us and directed it instead on His own Son. It is His *righteous* anger. He will not let injustice go unpunished. If He turns away His anger, it must go somewhere. And it fell on Jesus at the cross.

On a number of times in Hosea, he switches from warnings of judgment to promises of salvation in a moment. It startles you. You wonder if you have misread his words. How can Hosea be proclaiming judgment and then almost in the next breath be promising blessing beyond imagining? And the answer is that judgment *does* come on God's people, but it falls on Jesus in our place. God's anger, as it were, is bearing down on us, coming to crush us. But before it reaches us, God turns it away and on to the cross. And Christ absorbs the terrible force of God's anger in full. Father and Son co-operate together at the cross to avert their anger from us – if we turn to Jesus.

What is the result of God's turning?

1. We will flourish (14:5-6)
Much of Hosea's message has been, 'Turn, for in front of you is destruction. If you carry on along this path, you will be destroyed.' But here at the climax his message is, 'Turn, for behind you is God. If you change direction, then you will be heading along a path that leads to flourishing.'

> ⁵I will be like the dew to Israel;
>   he shall blossom like the lily;
>   he shall take root like the trees of Lebanon;
> ⁶his shoots shall spread out;
>   his beauty shall be like the olive,
>   and his fragrance like Lebanon.

I will be like the dew to Israel is not much of a promise in Sheffield, where I live. We do not suffer a lack of precipitation. But imagine living in a place where it did not rain for months on end. Then the promise of dew has real meaning. Maybe you feel *spiritually* dry. Hosea's invitation is, 'Look to God to be your dew, your refreshment, your renewal. Turn, come home to God and He will be like dew to you. And you will blossom like a flower. You will grow as a person. You will be splendid and fragrant. There will be something beautiful and refreshing about you.'

His shoots shall spread out in verse 6 is literally 'his shoots shall come.' It refers to new growth in a previously dead stump. Once we were spiritually dead (Eph. 2:1-3). But now God has made us alive and so we begin to spread life.

2. Other people will flourish through us (14:7)
Not only will we flourish, but other people will flourish through us:

> They shall return and dwell beneath my shadow;
>   they shall flourish like the grain;
> they shall blossom like the vine;
>   their fame shall be like the wine of Lebanon.

When Hosea says **they shall return and dwell beneath my shadow,** he is *not* saying that Israel will dwell beneath God's shadow. It is Israel whose shadow will shade people. It is important to follow the train of thought through from verse 5:

I [God] will be like the dew to Israel; he [Israel] shall blossom like the lily ... he shall ... his shoots will ... his beauty ... his fragrance ... his shade ... All the way through 'his' refers to Israel once Israel has been nourished by the dew of God. So the promise here is that the nations will dwell in the shade of Israel.

It is the same idea in the next line: **they shall flourish like the grain.** The meaning is probably 'they (like) grain shall sustain (people)'. In other words, Israel will bring life to the world. **Their fame** is literally Israel's 'remembrance'. When the nations remember Israel, when they think about Israel, they will do so with fondness like you might remember the taste of a good wine.

When we turn to God in repentance and faith, He not only makes *us* flourish, he makes *other people* flourish *through us*. It is a missional promise. God is promising to use us to provide shade and protection for people. He is promising to make us a source of life to people as we live and proclaim the gospel of Jesus. Or think about the people who have influenced your Christian life. Do you not remember them with fondness? Well, Hosea is promising that you can be one of those people, someone people remember with fondness. Your church can be a community that makes your neighbourhood flourish, a community who brings eternal life to people through the gospel.

If you want your church to flourish and to enable others to flourish, then do not start by 'doing' mission. Start by turning to God in daily repentance and faith. Look to Him as your Father. Point one another to Him as a Father. Why? Because God will make us flourish like nothing else can.

3. God will make us flourish like nothing else can (14:8)

> O Ephraim, what have I to do with idols?
> > It is I who answer and look after you.
> I am like an evergreen cypress;
> > from me comes your fruit.

What God is saying in effect is that He is superior to any alternative. There is no comparison. Lebanon has been mentioned three times in this song of God's turning:

- he shall take root like the trees of Lebanon (14:5);

- his beauty shall be like the olive, and his fragrance like Lebanon (14:6);

- their fame shall be like the wine of Lebanon (14:7).

The ESV and NIV add the words 'trees' or 'a cedar' in verse 5 and the NIV adds a 'cedar' in verse 6. But literally it is 'he shall take root like Lebanon' and 'his fragrance like Lebanon'. The focus is on Lebanon itself. The reason is that Baal worship came from Lebanon. It was introduced to Israel through Jezebel, the daughter of Ethbaal, the priest-king of Sidon, which is now Lebanon (1 Kings 16:31-33).

The people thought that if they followed Baal they could flourish like Lebanon. But Hosea is taking the language of Baal worship and subverting it. All the blessings that Israel thought would came from Baal will in fact come from God. They hoped Baal worship would make them like Lebanon, the home of Baal worship. But it is God who will make them truly fruitful.

Think back to the way you completed those sentences: 'I will be happy when ...' and 'My future will be secure if ...' These things will not satisfy, not in a lasting way. And they will not make you secure, not in the face of death.

But God is saying, 'Whatever you think these things will do for you, I will surpass it. I am the one who can truly make you flourish.' **It is I who answer and look after you** (14:8).

What does this mean? It does not mean guaranteed health and happiness, not in this life. But if you turn to God day by day, then God promises you this: joy in the midst of suffering; confidence in the face of guilt; contentment in every circumstance; freedom in the midst of constraint; peace in the midst of problems; love in the midst of rejection; strength in the midst of weakness. Above all, it means eternal life, secure in a new creation where there is no more death or mourning or crying or pain. You can flourish if you turn to God.

Let them understand (14:9)

Think back over what we have seen in the book of Hosea.

Our unfaithfulness. Hosea has told the story of Israel's unfaithfulness and not only Israel's unfaithfulness, but that of all humanity. We are all like an adulterous bride who turns away from God's love to other lovers who use and abuse us.

God's righteous judgment. Hosea has told the story of God's judgment against Israel and not only against Israel but against all humanity. We have provoked God's jealous anger. God would come against Israel, as He did when the Assyrian army defeated and destroyed the northern tribes, wiping them off the pages of history. And God is coming against us in judgment.

God's passionate love. But Hosea has also told the story of God's continuing love for His people. We see the heart of God exposed, raw, wounded, tender, passionate. And, because of His love, God calls us His children. 'Say to your brothers, "You are my people," and to your sisters, "You have received mercy"' (2:1).

What are you going to do with this message? Hosea offers a postscript to his message. It is a call to respond to his words wisely. It was perhaps added as a call to apply and reapply Hosea's message with wisdom in subsequent situations. So it is a word directly to us!

> Whoever is wise, let him understand these things;
>   whoever is discerning, let him know them;
> for the ways of the LORD are right,
>   and the upright walk in them,
>   but transgressors stumble in them. (14:9)

The wise thing to do is to acknowledge the truth of Hosea's message. **The ways of the LORD are right**. But there is more to wisdom than knowledge or mere assent. The wise thing to do is to walk in the ways of the LORD – to put God's Word into practice (Matt. 7:24-27 and James 1:22-25).

The word **stumble** in verse 9 is a repeat of the word in verse 1: **you have stumbled because of your iniquity**. If you have stumbled because of sin, it is not too late. **Take with you words and return to the LORD** (14:2).

STUDY QUESTIONS

1. What are the different ways that Hosea uses the term 'turn' or 'repent' in chapter 14?

2. Who do you remember with fondness because of the way God used them to bless you?

3. How could you be one of these people whom God uses to be a blessing to others?

4. Wisdom involves applying what we know so that we walk in the ways of the LORD. What does it mean to walk in the knowledge that we have been unfaithful?

5. What does it mean to walk in the knowledge of God's righteous anger that is coming?

6. What does it mean to walk in the knowledge that God calls us His children?

7. How has God spoken to you through the message of Hosea?

Questions for Personal Reflection

1. Review again how you would complete these sentences: 'I will really be happy when ...' and 'My future will be secure if ...'

2. Hosea invites you to 'take with you words'. What words will you bring to God? Compose your own 'liturgy of turning'. Ensure that you ask for forgiveness, renounce false security and express your faith in God's fatherly love.

3. Find time to pray through Hosea 14. Read a verse at a time and turn it into a prayer that you might be refreshed by the living God.

Subject Index

Scripture Index

Focus on the Bible Commentaries

Genesis: The Beginning of God's Plan of Salvation – Richard P. Belcher
ISBN 978-1-84550-963-7
Deuteronomy: The Commands of a Covenant God – Allan Harman
ISBN 978-1-84550-268-3

Joshua: No Falling Words – Dale Ralph Davis
ISBN 978-1-84550-137-2
Judges: Such a Great Salvation – Dale Ralph Davis
ISBN 978-1-84550-138-9

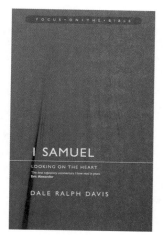

Ruth & Esther: God Behind the Seen – A. Boyd Luter/Barry C. Davis
ISBN 978-1-85792-805-9

1 Samuel: Looking on the Heart – Dale Ralph Davis
ISBN 978-1-85792-516-6

2 Samuel: Out of Every Adversity – Dale Ralph Davis
ISBN 978-1-84550-270-6

1 Kings The Wisdom and the Folly – Dale Ralph Davis
ISBN 978-1-84550-251-5

2 Kings: The Power and the Glory – Dale Ralph Davis
ISBN 978-1-84550-096-2

1 Chronicles: God's Faithfulness to the People of Judah – Cyril J. Barber
ISBN 978-1-85792-935-5

2 Chronicles: God's Blessing of His Faithful People – Cyril J. Barber
ISBN 978-1-85792-936-2

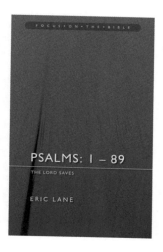

Job: Will You Torment a Windblown Leaf?– Bill Cotton
ISBN 978-1-85792-515-9

Psalms 1-89: The Lord Saves – Eric Lane
ISBN 978-1-84550-180-8

Psalms 90-150: The Lord Reigns – Eric Lane
ISBN 978-1-84550-202-7

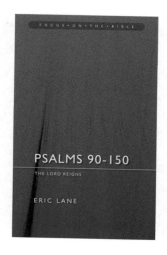

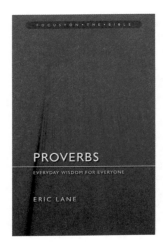

Proverbs: Everyday Wisdom for Everyone – Eric Lane
ISBN 978-1-84550-267-6

Ecclesiastes: The Philippians of the Old Testament – William D. Barrick
ISBN 978-1-84550-776-3

Song of Songs – James M. Hamilton
ISBN 978-1-78191-396-3
(coming late 2014)

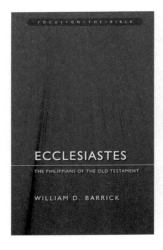

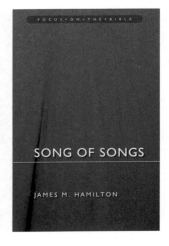

Isaiah: A Covenant to be Kept for the Sake of the Church – Allan Harman
ISBN 978-1-84550-053-5

Jeremiah and Lamentations: The Death of a Dream, and What Came After – Michael Wilcock
ISBN 978-1-78191-148-8

Daniel: A Tale of Two Cities – Robert Fyall
ISBN 978-1-84550-194-5

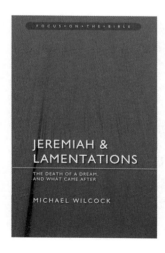
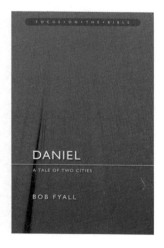

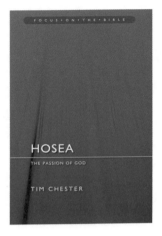

Hosea: The Passion of God – Tim Chester
ISBN 978-1-78191-368-0

Amos: An Ordinary Man with an Extraoridinary Message – T. J. Betts
ISBN 978-1-84550-727-5

Jonah, Michah, Nahum, Habakkuk & Zephaniah – John L. Mackay
ISBN 978-1-85792-392-6

Haggai, Zechariah & Malachi: God's Restored People – John L. Mackay
ISBN 978-1-85792-067-3

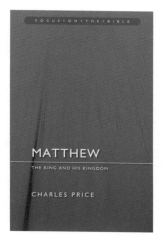

Matthew: The King and His Kingdom – Charles Price
ISBN 978-1-78191-146-4

Mark: Good News from Jerusalem – Geoffrey Grogan
ISBN 978-1-85792-905-8

Acts: Witnesses to Him – Bruce Milne
ISBN 978-1-84550-507-3

Romans: The Revelation of God's Righteousness – Paul Barnett
ISBN 978-1-84550-269-0

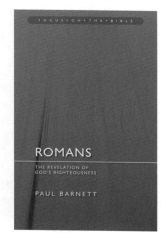

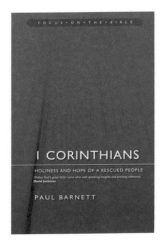

1 Corinthians: Holiness and Hope of a Rescued People – Paul Barnett
ISBN 978-1-84550-721-3

*2 Corinthians: The Glories & Responsibilities of Christian Servi*ce – Geoffrey Grogan
ISBN 978-1-84550-252-2

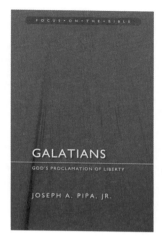

Galatians: God's Proclamation of Liberty – Joseph A. Pipa Jr.
ISBN 978-1-84550-558-5

Ephesians: Encouragement and Joy in Christ – Paul Gardner
ISBN 978-1-84550-264-5

Philippians: Rejoicing and Thanksgiving – David Chapman
ISBN 978-1-84550-687-2

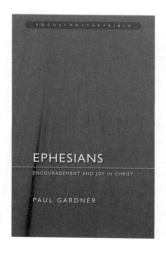

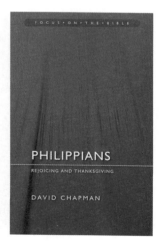

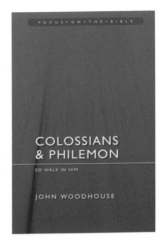

Colossians & Philemon: So Walk in Him – John Woodhouse
ISBN 978-1-84550-632-2

1 & 2 Thessalonians: Triumphs and Trials of a Consecrated Church – Richard Mayhue
ISBN 978-1-85792-452-7

1 & 2 Timothy & Titus – Douglas Milne
ISBN 978-1-85792-169-4

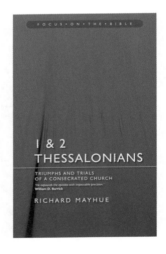

James: Wisdom for the Community – Christopher W. Morgan/B. Dale Ellenburg
ISBN 978-1-84550-335-2

1 & 2 Peter & Jude: Christian Living in an Age of Suffering – Paul Gardner
ISBN 978-1-78191-129-7

1, 2 & 3 John – Michael Eaton
ISBN 978-1-85792-152-6

Revelation: The Compassion and Protection of Christ – Paul Gardner
ISBN 978-1-84550-344-4

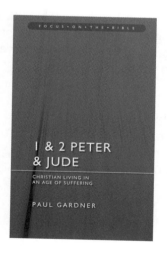

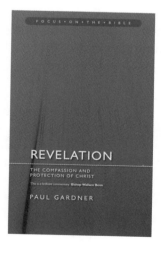

Christian Focus Publications

Our mission statement –

STAYING FAITHFUL
In dependence upon God we seek to impact the world through literature faithful to His infallible Word, the Bible. Our aim is to ensure that the Lord Jesus Christ is presented as the only hope to obtain forgiveness of sin, live a useful life and look forward to heaven with Him.

Our books are published in four imprints:

CHRISTIAN
FOCUS

Popular works including biographies, commentaries, basic doctrine and Christian living.

CHRISTIAN
HERITAGE

Books representing some of the best material from the rich heritage of the church.

MENTOR

Books written at a level suitable for Bible College and seminary students, pastors, and other serious readers. The imprint includes commentaries, doctrinal studies, examination of current issues and church history.

CF4•K

Children's books for quality Bible teaching and for all age groups: Sunday school curriculum, puzzle and activity books; personal and family devotional titles, biographies and inspirational stories – because you are never too young to know Jesus!

Christian Focus Publications Ltd,
Geanies House, Fearn, Ross-shire,
IV20 1TW, Scotland, United Kingdom.
www.christianfocus.com